When God Breathes

The Attributes of the Godhead

PASTOR JOSH MORGAN

WESTBOW
PRESS®
A DIVISION OF THOMAS NELSON
& ZONDERVAN

WestBow Press books may be ordered through booksellers or by contacting:

WestBow Press
A Division of Thomas Nelson & Zondervan
1663 Liberty Drive
Bloomington, IN 47403
www.westbowpress.com
1 (866) 928-1240

ISBN: 978-1-9736-7996-7 (sc)
ISBN: 978-1-9736-7997-4 (e)

Print information available on the last page.

WestBow Press rev. date: 01/06/2019

Contents

Foreword

In 1 Corinthians 2, we discover that the Holy Spirit is the only person on the planet that truly knows the deep things of God. Yet, because He is living on the inside of every believer in Jesus Christ, we are invited into a divine partnership with Him where we get to join Him on His own search of understanding the mysteries and revelation of God Himself. What profound and delightful news for you and I. We do not have to exercise our faith in our own strength. What relief and joy it brings to my soul!

As I sat reading this manuscript you are about to greatly enjoy, I kept thinking to myself that it could have only been written with the divine partnership of the Holy Spirit. With insightful teaching and practical application, Joshua Morgan opens up the eyes of our hearts to the role that the Father, Son, and Holy Spirit play in our lives. In fact, several times I had to pause while reading because an internal dialogue was stirred up in the depths of my heart as I processed what Joshua was revealing to us through the Word of God. One of my favorite things about this book is that it not only contains a realm of scholarship that is hard to find these days but it is also reader friendly regardless of where you are at in your walk with Christ. I would recommend this book to the seasoned saint as well as to the new believer.

I had the privilege of ministering at the church that Joshua and his wife pastor in West Virginia. Many men claim to possess knowledge and understanding, but few are willing to pay the price to acquire it. When I visit the congregation, I found a healthy and vibrant church that is passionate about the things of God. They love the movement of the Holy Spirit and it is evident that the leadership is committed to the place of prayer and intimacy with the Father.

It is my honor to commend not only this book to you, but this man of God to you. I can now say from personal experience that this manuscript is not written from the place of theory, but a practical outworking of all the years Joshua Morgan has spent in the ministry. He is a humble servant well capable of leading but the posture of a student that he takes causes him to stand out in this generation.

Prepare to be encouraged and activated as you read this tremendous work. I know I was!

-Jeremiah Johnson

Founder and Overseer of Heart of the Father Ministry
Best Selling Author
www.jeremiahjohnson.tv

1

~

When God Breathes - The Father

Everything God has done and will do is extravagant and has great purpose. All His actions have a planned objective, even the breath He breathes. Breathing is so routine that we do it every day of our lives without thought. We only seem to think of it when the air we inhale and exhale is interrupted. Life is granted with each breath we take. Without the fresh oxygen going in and out of our lungs, we would die. It goes without saying that breathing is essential to living. Imagine God breathing well-timed breaths one after the other. Each breath having purpose as He draws air in and expels it. Each breath could be as calm as a summer breeze or as mighty as a hurricane. We are talking about the God who refers to the earth as His footstool. Now take a moment and peacefully draw air into and expel it from your lungs. The act of breathing is the evidence of life. When God breathes, a miraculous and supernatural occurrence takes place. The Bible gives detail of what takes place when God the Father, the Son, and the Holy Spirit breathes. This book is a spirit prompted attempt to describe the purpose of God breathing. Transformation takes place when the Godhead breathes. When God the Father breathes, life is given. When God the Son breathes, salvation is granted. When God the Holy Spirit breathes, supernatural power is imparted.

The book of Genesis tells us that the earth was void and without form. Darkness covered all of creation because life was yet to exist. God spoke and all of creation came into existence. At His Word the world was formed. At His spoken Word, the hills, valleys, oceans, trees, animals, and all inhabitants of this planet came into being, at His breathed word. Words are carried by the air breathed in and out of our lungs.

> **(Psalms 33:6-7 NLT)** *"The Lord merely spoke, and the heavens were created, He breathed the word, and all the stars were born. He assigned the sea its boundaries and locked the oceans in vast reservoirs."*

The magnificence of God is unfathomable to the human mind. His abilities are not bound to the comprehension of man's wisdom or imagination. He is immeasurable, limitless and endless. He is not confined to man's thinking and understanding. He is time and He has no duration because He is the beginning and the end, the Alpha and the Omega.

God spoke all things into existence and declared it to be good.

> **(Genesis 1:31 NKJV)** *"Then God saw everything that He had made, and indeed it was very good."*

God was pleased with the creation He had spoken and breathed into existence.

The Making of Man

(Genesis 1:26-27 NKJV) *26. "Then God said, Let Us make man in Our image, according to our likeness; let them have dominion over the fish of the sea, over the birds of the air, and over the cattle, over all the earth and over every creeping thing that creeps on the earth. 27. So God created man in His image; in the image of God He created him; male and female He created them."*

Man was not spoken into existence like every other thing created by God. Man was intricately and personally designed by the Godhead. God, the three in one, formed and made man in the very likeness and image of the creator. Man is purposed to have dominion over all the earth and everything on it. Man is destined to reign as helmsman over creation.

(Genesis 1:26 AMP) *"Then God said, let us − Father, Son, Holy Spirit, make man in Our image, according to Our likeness [not physical, but a spiritual personality and moral likeness]; and let them have complete authority"*
(Genesis 2:7 NKJV) *"And the Lord God formed man of the dust of the ground, and breathed into his nostrils the breath of life; and man became a living being."*

Unlike the rest of creation, man required the intimacy of touch. Man is God's self-expression and workmanship. God carefully and meticulously formed man with His hands, leaving His fingerprints all over the perfect project. Every cell, molecule, and DNA treated as a delicacy. Man was created differently than anything else spoken by God. The creation of man required God's personal touch. The

3

importance of man's meticulous creation tells of God's desired destiny. Man is the trophy produced from the master potter's touch, formed from the dust of the ground. Destined to be caretaker and groundskeeper of all creation. Man is to exist with creation while having authority and dominion over it.

Man was God's prized and personal creation, but he did not contain life. The created man was perfect, but not a living creation because he had not been breathed upon. Once God was pleased with the creation, He breathed into his nostrils the breath of life. Not until he was breathed on did man become a living soul. The breath of God brings life. The portrait of man's destiny becomes clearer in the picture of God's intimate breathing. My mind attempts to imagine the Godhead closely looking over the careful design. My imagination sees God face to face with this new product. Once God approves, He comes nose to nose and breathes into the nostrils of man. God breathing grants life to this lifeless creation. God breathing now gives the same created freedom to man that was given to the rest of creation. Perfection cannot be rushed.

> **(Psalm 139:14 NIV)** *"I praise you because I am fearfully and wonderfully made; your works are wonderful, I know that full well."*

When God breathes, life is granted.
When God the Father Breathes, it gives life.

Dry Bones Come Alive

The text from Ezekiel 37:1-14 has been vastly studied and several points demand discussion. Our focus is on the life-giving breath of God. Like that of man's creation, we see the renewing formation of

4

mankind. Through the prophesying of Ezekiel these dead lifeless bones came together and formed human bodies. Like Adam, they were still lifeless because they were not breathing.

> **(Ezekiel 37:8–10 NKJV)** *8. "Indeed, as I looked, the sinews and the flesh came upon them, and the skin covered them over; but there was no breath in them. 9. Also He said to me, prophesy, son of man, and say to the breath, thus says the Lord God: come from the four winds, O breath, and breathe on these slain, that they may live. 10. So I prophesied as He commanded me, and breath came into them, and they lived, and stood upon their feet, an exceedingly great army."*

The Hebrew word "ruah" can be translated breath, wind, or spirit. Once again, life required the breath of God. In this text, the breath is transported by the four winds. The four winds either represent the four quarters of the earth or God's omnipresence. After the dry bones became fleshly bodies they were breathed upon and stood as an exceedingly great army. The text, "I will put My Spirit in you" in verse 14 is the same Hebrew "ruah" as in verse 8. The human body is subordinate to the breath of God. Inferior in its design so that God gets glory for the life sustained in it. Though we have bones with marrow, bodies with skin and organs, it is the presence and breath of God that grants life. God breathed and a valley of lifeless bodies stood to their feet, an exceedingly great army. I picture a large military brigade abruptly standing at attention. The breath of God had caused life to enter their bodies.

The Word – Divine Inspiration

(2 Timothy 3:16 NKJV) *"All scripture is given by inspiration of God, and is profitable for doctrine, for reproof, for correction, for instruction in righteousness."*

All scripture is divinely birthed and inspired from God and the scripture is the absolute authority over the lives of believers. This verse may be small, but it gives the actual process of the Word coming to life. Through study you will find the Greek word for "Inspiration of God," Theopneustos, literally means "God-Breathed." The derivation of the Word, or the Bible, is God breathed. The Spirit of God breathed on human instruments as they penned each word and thought as directed by God Himself. The Bible was not birthed from an entrepreneur mindset or idea. The Holy Scripture contained in the Bible transcends the wisdom and competence of those who authored the greatest collection of words ever written. Once we remove the concept that the Bible was written through human intellect, we conceive it was intentionally birthed when God breathed. Sixty-six books written by forty authors over more than four thousand years in three different original languages. All forty authors moved by the breath of God to write, as He gave them direction.

(2 Timothy 3:16 NIV) *"All scripture is God-breathed and is useful for teaching, rebuking, correcting and training in righteousness."*

(English Standard Version) *"All scripture is breathed out by God and profitable for teaching, for reproof, for correction, and for training in righteousness."*

None of what was written belongs to the private opinion of the writers. Each writer and author were moved and inspired by the Holy Spirit. God perfectly planned and allowed many of the authors to have specific experiences for bringing their personal stories to life in fulfillment of the scripture. This biblical view of the Bible's derivation is called the "plenary verbal inspiration" of Scripture, meaning every word is inspired by the Holy Spirit of God. Inspired Scripture is simply written revelation. The "Verbal" means the Bible in its original languages, is an exact record of the mind and will of God as He intended it to be. "Plenary" means the entire text of the Bible is equally from God, complete in every way, lacking nothing. And "Inspiration" means God-breathed. Many scholars believe you must study the Bible in its original languages to fully understand the mysteries within. The writers of this Holy book would tell us that human intelligence does not play a part in fulfilling the Will of God. When God is breathing, anything is possible. God chose, inspired and sovereignly guided the biblical authors who were equipped by Him to write the very words of scripture.

> **(2 Peter 1:20-21 NKJV)** *"20. Knowing this first, that no prophecy of scripture is of any private interpretation, 21. for prophecy never came by the will of man, but holy men of God spoke as they were moved by the Holy Spirit."* This revelation alone demands our precepts to change. Reading your Bible can no longer be a passing of time duty or Bible study obligation. The Word is God breathing. Every time you read and quote Scripture you transfer the power of God through His words.

> **(Hebrews 4:12 NKJV)** *"For the word of God is living and powerful, and sharper than any two-edged sword, piercing even to the division of soul and spirit, and of the joints and marrow, and is a discerner of the thoughts and intents of the heart."*

The Scripture is a living breathing document meant to reveal God's truths. To receive God's word, we must confess God's word. The Greek term for Word here is "Logos." It indicates the expression of a complete idea and is used in referring to Scripture. The Scripture is actively alive and powerfully reaching into the depths of man, even the hidden areas, discerning the heart of man. The God breathed Word never slumbers nor sleeps. The reign of living "Logos" is the source of power and life for the believer.

His Word Will Live Forever

> **(1 Peter 1:25a NKJV)** *"But the word of the Lord endures forever."*

> **(Matthew 24:35 NKJV)** *"Heaven and earth will pass away, but My words will by no means pass away."*

> **(Isaiah 55:11 NKJV)** *"So shall My word be that goes forth from My mouth; it shall not return to Me void, but it shall accomplish what I please, and it shall prosper in the thing for which I sent it.*

> **(Psalms 119:89 NKJV)** *"Forever, O Lord, your word is settled in heaven."*

2

The Gifts of the Father

Many books have been written about the promised blessings of
God. Believers who have found these promises true live in peace
and victory no matter what life sets before them. They can do this
because they know and trust that all good gifts and good things are
from God.

> **(James 1:17 NIV)** *"Every good and perfect gift is from
> above, coming down from the Father of heavenly lights, who
> does not change like shifting shadows."*

God has left nothing incomplete. His gifts are endless, and His
promised blessings are innumerable. The gifts of the Godhead are
a study of gifts given by the Father, the Son, and the Holy Spirit. It
may surprise you to know that God has already planned and prepared
to give you everything you need to obtain success and victory. The
gifts of the Father are for every believer. Given without prejudice or

favoritism, God wants all His children to be equipped with His gifts. Let's review the spiritual and ministry gifts given by God the Father.

> **(Romans 12:3–8 NKJV)** *For I say, through the grace given to me, to everyone who is among you, not to think of himself more highly than he ought to think, but to think soberly, as God has dealt to each one a measure of faith. For as we have many members in one body, but all the members do not have the same function, so we, being many, are one body in Christ, and individually members of one another. Having then gifts differing according to the grace that is given to us, let us use them: if prophecy, let us prophesy in proportion to our faith; or ministry, let us use it in our ministering; he who teaches, in teaching; he who exhorts, in exhortation; he who gives, with liberality; he who leads, with diligence; he who shows mercy, with cheerfulness.*

We have many members in one body and not all members have the same function. But all members are of the same body and have been given faith to operate in the gifts mentioned. These gifts will not function the same in every believer. Like the nine Spiritual gifts, the Father's gifts will have diversities of activities and operate differently in each believer. We read that God has granted every believer to function in these seven gifts. In order, the gifts listed are prophecy, ministry, teaching, exhortation, giving, leading, and showing mercy. Let's examine the seven gifts of the Father individually.

1. Prophecy

The Father's gift of prophecy is revelation in Godly wisdom and Word. The ability to share gained knowledge and wisdom with those ready to hear. This prophecy is to speak with insight and revelation. As a believer grows they learn things in the Word and gain biblical revelation that is meant to be shared with others. Any time you share a gained revelation by the Spirit in the Word you are prophesying. Many times, when preachers are preaching or teachers are teaching the Spirit will reveal something new to them from scripture. This revelatory impartation shared is the Father's gift of prophecy. Below is a set of scriptures showing how people came to a revelation and shared what they learned. Again, this gift of prophecy is for all believers.

> **(Matthew 16:15–17 NKJV)** *15. He said to them, But who do you say that I am? 16. Simon Peter answered and said, "You are the Christ, the son of the living God." 17. Jesus answered and said to him, "Blessed are you, Simon Bar-Jonah, for flesh and blood has not revealed this to you, but my Father who is in heaven."*

> **(John 4:29 NKJV)** *Come, see a man who told me all things that I ever did. Could this be the Christ?*

Note: Prophesy-Prophet-Prophecy. Gifts of the Father, the Son, and the Holy Spirit all involve a form of prophecy, so it's necessary to briefly detail the differences. The Fathers motivation gift of prophecy belongs to all flesh, operating from gained knowledge. The Holy Spirits gift of prophecy is a verbal supernatural prompting from the Spirit. Specifically, a word delivered by the Spirit through the believer. The Son's office gift of the prophet speaks of a leader ordained and consecrated to give detailed specific Spirit led messages. Three similar gifts, yet completely different in operation.

2. Ministry

Ministry is like that of the office of a deacon. The ministry is to perform service and to serve the people of God. If you are willing to render general everyday services in love then you are fulfilling this gift. This gift is also compatible to that of the ministry of helps. God has so perfectly designed His creation that He left out no details. Fulfilling the large and small needs of the saints. The gift of ministry and helps may seem small in value but they are the glue that holds churches and ministries together. When I think of ministry I think of the wonderful people who retrieve our attendance sheets at the end of service. These folks have never been asked to do this nor do they gain accolades. Their service in doing so is a great blessing to our staff.

3. Teaching

Teaching is the supernatural ability to reveal and explain the mysteries of God's Word. A good teacher carries the charismatic gift of communication. This teaching is the impartation of the gained knowledge in the Word of God. This gift makes clear the truths learned and educates the listener. The teaching of the Word will often use the above gift of prophecy in giving biblical truths.

4. Exhortation

The call to encourage the body of Christ both in action and word. Using ones influence to bring comfort. It should be our goal to bring uplifting words to build the body. Exhortation takes place when believers expel envy and strife bringing encouraged unity.

> **(Proverbs 18:21 NKJV)** *"Death and life are in the power of the tongue."*

Words spoken can literally grant life to the hearer. Our words can also bring death and destruction to the hearer. Encouraging exhortation is vital to the success of believers seeking to be one body in Christ. For too long the enemy has been given permission to use our tongues as a devastating tool to destroy and tear down other believers. God purposed to place exhortation as an important gift so that we would take priority in being Christlike.

> **(Hebrew 10:25 NKJV)** *"not forsaking the assembling of ourselves together, as in the manner of some, but exhorting one another, and so much the more as you see the day approaching."*

God purposed fellowship to be part of the church's doctrine so that each time we come together we can build each other up.

5. Giving

A giving Spirit is a Godly Spirit. A generously giving Christian is a Christlike Christian. About this time many people will turn the page looking for more lenient and pleasant reading. If you seek to bypass the God given gift of giving, then you do not have the Spirit of a giver. Having the gift of giving is one of God's more extravagant gifts to His children. Most never think of giving as a gift but without it many needs would go unmet. This gift of giving is above tithing and refers to one giving generously out of their resources to meet the needs of the church and others. Givers do so without pride and they do so not seeking anything in return. The church needs more givers, and I'm not only referring to tithers. This gift is beyond tithing. This specifically refers to people meeting the needs of others and the church out of their abundant resources. A willingness to give what God has blessed you with. I recently read Robert Morris's book, "The Blessed Life," and I would highly recommend that you read this book about the subject of giving.

> **(2 Corinthians 8:2 NLT)** *"They are being tested by many troubles, and they are very poor. But they are also filled with abundant joy, which has overflowed in rich generosity."*

> **(2 Corinthians 9:11, 13 NLT)** *11. "Yes, you will be enriched in every way so that you can always be generous. And when we take your gifts to those who need them, they will thank God." 13. As a result of your ministry, they will give glory to God. For your generosity to them and to all believers will prove that you are obedient to the Good News of Christ."*

In many ways, generosity has become a stranger to the Christian faith. The goal for the gift of giving is to teach His children not to be selfish or penurious. In doing so, we meet the needs of other saints. Imagine a day when believer's needs are met without asking because of the generosity of others. It's important to note that to receive you must first give.

(Galatians 6:7 NKJV) *"For whatever a man sows, that he will also reap."*

6. Leadership

At the heart of leadership is influence. Those who lead are gifted and anointed to do so. Leaders are those who have the influence to have others follow. This gift describes those who stand in front modeling with Christlike character developed by the Holy Spirit. All leaders are first disciples and servants. Good leaders remain disciples and servants.

(Matthew 20:26 NKJV) *"But whoever desires to become great among you, let him be your servant."*

Leadership does not always mean power. Biblical leadership is the ability to influence, guide, and direct. There are different levels of leadership with different levels of influence. Godly leaders obtain willing followers, not forced or obligated followers.

(Mark 10:45 NKJV) *"For even the Son of Man did not come to be served, but to serve, and to give His life a ransom for many."*

7. Mercy

Grace declares that we as adopted children have been given mercy. The same measure of mercy received should be the same measure you give. The love of God transcends all our past sin and current shortcomings. This is the mercy we are expected to extend to others in need. To feel sympathy for others by relating in love and respect. This gift is to be given with kindness, cheerfulness, and sometimes forgiveness. God granted us grace willingly, and not as a matter of duty. We are to offer the same mercy and grace willingly.

(Matthew 7:12 NKJV) *"Whatever you want men to do to you, do also to them."* **(Luke 10:27–37 The Good Samaritan)**

Christian – It's More Than a Word

(Acts 11:26 NIV) *"The disciples were called Christians first at Antioch."*

The church had finally grown so much the world needed to label this group, so they called them Christians. The label of Christian literally meant you were Christlike. From that day until now followers of Jesus are still called Christian. My prayer is that we realize the title is more than a word. It should describe character rather than church attendance. We just concluded a great segment describing the gifts given to believers by the Father. Those gifts are given for the benefit of the people and they should lead us to represent the likeness of the God who gave the gifts. The verses listed below, following the gifts of the Father tell what we should look like when we operate as sons and daughters of the most high God.

(Romans 12:9-21 KNJV) *"9 Let love be without hypocrisy. Abhor what is evil. Cling to what is good. 10 Be kindly affectionate to one another with brotherly love, in honor giving preference to one another; 11 not lagging in diligence, fervent in spirit, serving the Lord; 12 rejoicing in hope, patient in tribulation, continuing steadfastly in prayer; 13 distributing to the needs of the saints, given to hospitality. 14 Bless those who persecute you; bless and do not curse. 15 Rejoice with those who rejoice, and weep with those who weep. 16 Be of the same mind toward one another. Do not set your mind on high things, but associate with the humble. Do not be wise in your own opinion. 17 Repay no one evil for evil. Have regard for good things in the sight of all men. 18 If it is possible, as much as depends on you, live peaceably with all men. 19 Beloved, do not avenge yourselves, but rather give place to wrath; for it is written, "Vengeance is Mine, I will repay," says the Lord. 20 Therefore, "If your enemy is hungry, feed him; If he is thirsty, give him a drink; For in so doing you will heap coals of fire on his head." 21 Do not be overcome by evil, but overcome evil with good."*

These verses willingly tell the testimony of believers without words being spoken. Reading those scriptures over and over will demand the Christlike Christian character to arise and represent the Savior who died that we may have life. Do you see yourself when you read the detailed prerequisite of Christian behavior? Do you love without hypocrisy? Are you kind in putting others before yourself? Are you serving the Lord in all diligence while rejoicing each day even if tribulation comes, praying continually? Do you give generously to other saints while extending the hand of hospitality? Do you bless those who come against you? Are you humble in your words while trying to respectfully get along with others? Do you struggle with revenge or are you at peace with those who bless you and those who curse you? It's one thing to be a blessing to those you call friend, but can you do the same for those you consider as an enemy? Does evil contend for your thoughts or is your mind and body under subjection to the will of the Father? To behave and live as a true Christian requires intentional and deliberate tendencies. Let's be honest, fulfillment of these scriptures takes work and often repentance. Over time one learns to crucify the flesh and its desires while giving the Spirit lead in how we conduct ourselves.

A Living Sacrifice

> **(Romans 12:1 NKJV)** *"I beseech you therefore, brethren, by the mercies of God, that you present your bodies a living sacrifice, holy, acceptable to God, which is your reasonable service."*

All things belonging to God are to be consecrated to Him, set apart and devoted to His cause. The Old Testament saints continually offered sacrifices to God as a way of honoring Him. From Genesis to Malachi we read of different animals being set apart and sanctified for sacrifice. Once Jesus was accepted as the acceptable sacrifice for our sins there was no more need for the sacrifice of animals. Atonement was now completed through Jesus Christ. God no longer sought the sacrifice of animals. He now longed for a more perfect and willing sacrifice. He seeks the living sacrifice of those redeemed by the ultimate sacrifice of His Son. The Christian life is built around the concept of sacrifice. The reasonably requested sacrifice is that of the living saints and maturing Christians who increasingly sacrifice their own desires and embrace His will, that we would present ourselves to Him consecrated and set apart. Submitting ourselves to the Lord requires a definite decision to give Him control and a daily commitment to remain under His authority. To be a living sacrifice means to dedicate yourself to the will of the Father, that's it. Living not to satisfy selfish ambitions but to live the purpose of pleasing the creator. This is a reasonable request pertaining to a season, being intentional each day to carry out the love and will of God, fulfilling the scripture in our daily walk. In the Old Testament, it was necessary for sacrifices to die. Under the New Covenant grace and sacrifice of Jesus, now it is required for sacrifices to live and live holy. Living a life pleasing to the Lord and by the scripture is considered a living sacrifice. Not only that, a living sacrifice will also exemplify the gifts of the Father. When one exemplifies the gifts of the Father by being a living sacrifice, they will excel in being a model Christlike Christian.

How Do You Measure Up?

This chapter discussed the gifts of the Father, the character of a Christian, and what it means to be a living sacrifice. Truth is, we must live all of Romans 12 to be successful with any part of it. It seems like a lot but, honestly, it's not that complicated. If you can study the scripture and live by it the best you can you'll grow more and more toward fulfilling its purpose. God is calling you to be more like Him and He knows you won't succeed overnight. However, He does expect effort and progress in the process. The best way to evaluate is to review the gifts and see how you measure up. As you read each one, examine your Christian walk and pray about where you are. Don't be too judgmental toward yourself. If you're falling short it's good to identify that area so you can begin the work to improve. Always start in prayer and reading the scripture. The seven gifts were prophecy, ministry, teaching, exhortation, giving, leadership and mercy. Remember, God wants all His children to operate in these gifts. Not necessarily in the same manner or to the same degree but using each gift as you are gifted to do so.

3

Glorious Identity

Your identity distinguishes individuality. Character, qualities, beliefs, and morals constitute the objective reality of a thing. Your identity tells the story of you; what you like, dislike, what you believe, what you enjoy, personalities you connect with, what makes you laugh, what makes you cry, what you stand for and what you stand against. You have a developed personality and identity. Every person on earth is born with a disposition. Your disposition is your temperamental makeup, prevailing tendency, mood, or inclination. Intentionally changed behavior over time is needed to reconstruct one's identity and to reshape one's disposition. What is your identity? What is your given disposition? How do others see you? Are you considerate to other people? Are you considered friendly? What kind of temper do you have? How would those who know you best describe your identity, in confidentiality, without you aware they were describing you? Identity can determine outcome and destiny. Accepting Jesus Christ as your savior can bring about a new identity. The Holy Spirit can take what's right and make it better or give you a new identity all together. A relationship with Jesus and being baptized in the Spirit requires a new identity. Change comes automatically. This scripture bears repeating,

> **(2 Corinthians 5:17 NKJV)** *"Therefore, if anyone is in Christ, he is a new creation; old things have passed away; behold, all things have become new."*

Christlike Identity

> **(2 Corinthians 3:18 NKJV)** *"But we all, with unveiled face, beholding as in a mirror the glory of the Lord, are being transformed into the same image from glory to glory, just as by the Spirit of the Lord."*

Man is created in the likeness and image of God. Why then would we need to be transformed? We were created in likeness visually. But transformation is also required for the inward invisible part of man. The body bears His likeness, the soul and spirit must be reborn and transformed into the same image. Believers should behold the glory of the Lord within themselves. We behold His revealed, "unveiled face," glory as if we are looking in a mirror. We are to see His glory when we look within ourselves. His reflection should be what we see when we gaze at our image. Not so much what we look like, but what our person, soul and Spirit is becoming. Self-evaluation should reveal the character and likeness of Christ. Complete Christlike identity doesn't happen immediately. We are transformed from glory to glory. There are multiple levels to the makeover. This makes sense once we realize that man is made of three parts, body, soul, and spirit. We are continually active to become more like Him.

To transform is to change in appearance, condition, nature, and character. True change means to be converted. It's much like the process off metamorphosis. The believer is to reflect the glory of the Lord just as Moses did. But the glory on Moses faded with time because it was temporary.

> **(Exodus 34:29-35 NKJV) V.35** *"And whenever the children of Israel saw the face of Moses, that the skin of Moses' face shown, then Moses would put the veil on his face again, until he went in to speak with Him."*

Moses had spent an extended amount of intimate time with God. Moses came down from Mount Sanai with God's glory literally glowing from his face. Again, the glory Moses experienced was temporary. New covenant salvation is a continuous change, from glory to glory. You get the point. Glorious transforming conversion takes place by the abiding presence of the Spirit of God. We are being changed with each new day, from glory to glory, from one level to another level, continuously. With ever increasing glory, we behold what we reflect.

> **(Romans 8:29 NKJV)** *"For whom He foreknew, He also predestined to be conformed to the image of His Son, that He might be the firstborn among many brethren."*

He knew us and predestined us before we were born. God's plans and purposes are eternal. Not confined in time or by time. He knows the end from the beginning.

> **(Jeremiah 1:5 NKJV)** *"Before I formed you in the womb I knew you; before you were born I sanctified you."*

We are destined to be the children of God. Predestined and preordained to be conformed to the image of His Son. 2 Corinthians 3:18 used the word transformed, while Romans 8:29 uses conformed. To conform is to become similar in form, nature, and character, and to act in harmony with prevailing standards, attitudes, and practices. Transformation changes the inward being of the man. Conforming is the manifestation of those changes. The objective is to become more and more like Christ. Jesus is the personification of who and what God wants us to embody. Jesus is the perfect reflection of the glory of God. His life and His being set the standard of the glorious identity. Love, mercy, righteousness, and holiness characterize the incarnate Jesus. If we are to become like Him, we must be transformed and conformed from glory to glory, continuously changing from one degree to another. Our aim and God's desire is Christlike identity. Others can't see it if you can't. You must first see His image within yourself before the world will see it.

> **(Galatians 2:20 NLT)** *"My old self has been crucified with Christ. It is no longer I who live, but Christ lives in me. So I live in this earthly body by trusting in the Son of God, who loved me and gave himself for me."*

Unveiled Glory

There are different levels and types of glory. Glory is not just heavenly but can be experienced on earth, made possible by the Spirit of God. We've already learned you can grow from glory to glory. Glory is defined many ways, such as praise or honor, the presence of God, beauty or splendor, a state of great gratification or exaltation, or distinguished qualities or assets. Biblical glory can be the description of God in all His majesty, the examination of God's work, the manifested presence of God, the revelation or revealing of God in His creation, the final glory revealed in the resurrected state of believers, and heaven.

> **(John 17:22 NLT)** *"I have given them the glory you gave me, so they may be one as we are one."*

> **(2 Corinthians 4:6 NLT)** *"For God, who said, "Let there be light in the darkness, has made this light shine in our hearts so we could know the glory of God that is seen in the face of Jesus Christ."*

The expressed love of God and His glory was given so that we may become one. God's glory, His majesty and His presence, has been gifted to man. Unveiled glory, revealed to the children of God.

> **(Matthew 27:50–51 NKJV)** *"50 And Jesus cried out again with a loud voice, and yielded up His spirit. 51 Then, behold, the veil of the temple was torn in two from top to bottom;"*

The death of Jesus repealed the separation of God and man. The veil had separated God from man and man from God's glory. When Jesus declared "it is finished" the veil was torn giving man complete access to the presence and glory of God. No longer would His glory be veiled causing a divide. The unveiled glory now abides in the reborn and redeemed lives of His children. His glory is in you, and His glory is you. When you became the container of His glory you became His glory. His Spirit in you, is His glory on you, unveiled, like looking into a mirror, beholding the glory of God.

(1 Corinthians 3:16 NKJV) *"Do you not know that you are the temple of God and that the Spirit of God dwells in you?"*

The glory of God in you begins at salvation and grows from glory to glory as you mature in God. His presence not only abides on earth, His presence abides in you.

(Romans 8:30 NKJV) *"Moreover who He predestined, these He also called; whom He called, these He also justified; and whom He justified, these He also glorified.*

God's plan is purposed and perfect. Tomorrow is a mystery to all except God. This text has four points. He predestined, called, justified, and glorified, the blueprint from beginning to end. We are chosen and foreordained for adoption to become sons and daughters of God. The call is a binding agreement to produce an intended outcome, free from sin and called to grace. The breath of the Son of God has freed us from sin's hold, declaring us righteous.

(Romans 3:24 NKJV) *"being justified freely by His grace through the redemption that is in Christ Jesus."*

The power of corruption broken in the effectual call. The guilt of sin removed in justification. The supernatural divine breath of Jesus brings one to glorification. Oneness and unity with the Godhead. Salvation brings transformation and conforms us to the image and likeness of Jesus Christ. He has glorified us in this temporary earthly body. He will complete the glorification at the rapture.

(2 Corinthians 3:7-18 NKJV) *"⁷ But if the ministry of death, written and engraved on stones, was glorious, so that the children of Israel could not look steadily at the face of Moses because of the glory of his countenance, which glory was passing away, ⁸ how will the ministry of the Spirit not be more glorious? ⁹ For if the ministry of condemnation had glory, the ministry of righteousness exceeds much more in glory. ¹⁰ For even what was made glorious had no glory in this respect, because of the glory that excels. ¹¹ For if what is passing away was glorious, what remains is much more glorious ¹² Therefore, since we have such hope, we use great boldness of speech— ¹³ unlike Moses, who put a veil over his face so that the children of Israel could not look steadily at the end of what was passing away. ¹⁴ But their minds were blinded. For until this day the same veil remains unlifted in the reading of the Old Testament, because the veil is taken away in Christ. But even to this day, when Moses is read, a veil lies on their heart. Nevertheless, when one turns to the Lord, the veil is taken away. Now the Lord is the Spirit; and where the Spirit of the Lord is, there is liberty. ¹⁸ But we all, with unveiled face, beholding as in a mirror the glory of the Lord, are being transformed into the same image from glory to glory, just as by the Spirit of the Lord."*

This text reveals the glory of the New Covenant along with the work and ministry of the Holy Spirit. The glory Moses experienced was temporary and covered with a veil. The New Covenant glory in Christ takes away the veil, transforming all who receive Jesus as Lord. "For if what is passing away was glorious, what remains is much more glorious." The glorious presence and Spirit of God is no longer hidden or separated from man.

Whole Unity

One theme remains constant in Scripture when discussing the breath of God and the gifts, unity. A divided body is a dysfunctional body. God desires the body to be many yet one, combining all parts in agreement and harmony. The perfect portrait of unity is the Godhead, three in one.

> **(Matthew 5:14 NKJV)** *"You are the light of the world. A city that is set on a hill cannot be hidden."*

Glory revealed in one believer multiplies in the union of the body of Christ creating a splendor that cannot be hidden. A unified body is a spiritually healthy body. The Spirit is bound and not free when the body is divided.

> **(Mark 3:25 NKJV)** *"And if a house is divided against itself, that house cannot stand."*

The Spirit is free and must remain so. He will not operate in a house disunited.

> **(Amos 3:3 NKJV)** *"Can two walk together, unless they are agreed?"*

From Genesis to Revelation, unity and oneness is the prerequisite for the outpouring of the Holy Spirit and presence of God.

4

~

Is the King Present

(Psalm 51:10-12 NKJV) *"Create in me a clean heart, O God, and renew a steadfast spirit within me. Do not cast me away from Your presence, and do not take Your Holy Spirit from me. Restore to me the joy of your salvation, and uphold me by your generous Spirit."*

David had witnessed the presence and Spirit of God being removed from Saul when he had sinned and refused to repent.

(1 Samuel 16:14 NKJV) *"But the Spirit of the Lord departed from Saul, and a distressing spirit from the Lord troubled him."*

Saul's experience of losing His presence was the beginning of the end for his reign. The only way that seems fitting to describe such an experience is to slowly lose the ability to breathe, asphyxiation. David's desperate plea details the importance of living every day in the intimacy of communal relationship with the Lord. The fear of being removed from courtship is not a risk David is willing to take nor does he desire to know what it's like not to be guided and loved by the presence of his Father.

> (**Psalm 16:11b NKJV**) *"In your presence is fullness of joy; at your right hand are pleasures evermore."*

David knew the joy and pleasure of being called and anointed by God the Father. He fully apprehended what it meant to be chosen by God. He knew the assurance that comes with being His son.

> (**1 Samuel 16:12-13 NKJV**) *"12. So he went and brought him in. Now he was ruddy, with bright eyes, and good looking. And the Lord said, Arise, anoint him; for this is the one! 13.Then Samuel took the horn of oil and anointed him in the midst of his brothers; and the Spirit of the Lord came upon David from that day forward."*

Surrounding David's plea is a prayer of cleansing to ensure that nothing will come between him and his God. David had been anointed by God and he constantly experienced Him at work in his life. He had been delivered more than once by God's grace and his desperate plea is a testimony to the goodness of his God. If we intend to be chosen as David was, we must recognize our need for His presence and His Spirit. O God, please do not remove us from your presence. O God, please do not take Your Holy Spirit from us.

I am now middle age and I've been serving the Lord since I was twelve years old. Attending church has been a normal part of life since I was in my mother's womb. I've been in more services, revivals, tent meetings, conferences and prayer services than I could dare to count. Countless times I have been in and witnessed His presence and His Spirit in mighty ways. I know what it's like to experience His glory personally and in meetings where His presence and Spirit find habitation. The glory of God is simply unexplainable. I've cried, lamented, praised, danced, fell prostrate, operated in spiritual gifts, and the list could continue to fill many pages. I'm privileged to have witnessed miracles, healings, transformations, and salvations. When I sit down to remember all that I've experienced it simply overwhelms me.

I was raised and found salvation in a Spirit filled church. Honestly, if a definition were needed to describe my upbringing it would fall under the charismatic Pentecostal category. We were obedient of anything and everything the Spirit led us to do. My parents were Pentecostal preachers and they continue that path today. Church was never boring and always filled with activities that led to great stories. My life was filled with spiritual services that could be told 2,000 years later like the church of Acts 2. When I became an adult and began to have a ministry of my own, I often would parallel the present to the past things I had been taught as a preacher's kid. Over time it became clear that I needed to make a shift into a new walk. As Oral Robert's taught, "methods may change but the message never changes." I needed to allow Holy Spirit to develop new methods and not imitate only what I had been taught and had learned over the years. Time and experience proved that God wasn't calling me to have a ministry that would imitate my parent's ministry. He was calling me into a new thing. My family and my church provided the foundation but now it was time to allow the Lord to build and grow my calling as it pleased Him. Even though many methods have changed, I know and recognize the one unchanging fact is the need for His Spirit and presence. In time, you learn that nothing can be accomplished without it. Many have tried, and all have failed. Every sign, every wonder, every salvation, and every spirit filled service has been accredited to the indwelling presence of God.

As I evaluate now, statistics would say that I've experienced success in ministry. I'm honored to report that I get to pastor the greatest group of spirit-filled believers and we frequently witness the moving of the Spirit. It is common to have multiple people receive salvation in our services. It is common to have our agenda overtaken by the Holy Spirit. I can say without doubt that we enter Covenant Church never really knowing the fullness of what God is about to do. I must tell you; it is very exciting to experience church where the Holy Spirit is expected to show up and show off. We have a great building, lots of parking, tremendous staff, our building and property are debt free and we are blessed to have a large diverse congregation. But now I must tell you the real truth, big buildings and big congregations are the least braggadocios words that I can write on paper. Without the Spirit, none of these outstanding achievements would matter. The greatest testimony to our church and our people is the continuous dwelling and moving of the Spirit of God. I can personally guarantee that if you come to our church you will experience that amazing Spirit of God. Our services are always filled with a spiritual intimacy that only the Holy Spirit can provide. Just as David declared, I declare as well. His presence is more precious than anything this world can offer. His presence is life changing.

> **(1 Corinthians 2:14 NLT)** *"But people who aren't spiritual can't receive these truths from God's Spirit. It all sounds foolish to them and they can't understand it, for only those who are spiritual can understand what the Spirit means."*

I tell you all of this to briefly mention a burden in my spirit. New statistics say churches are growing rapidly without the presence of God. I have witnessed this troubling movement myself. Pastors teaching the desire to have church without the disruption of the Holy Spirit or His gifts. Services structured to hold the Spirit clandestine and hidden out of sight from the attendees. Churches advertising calm and timely services without pressure and conviction. I weep over this new movement sweeping our land. I've been told how unnecessary it is to have services with freedom of Spirit. Although the Word declares,

(2 Corinthians 3:17 NKJV) *"Now the Lord is the Spirit: and where the Spirit of the Lord is, there is liberty."*

With my own ears, I've heard pastors teach why salvation altar calls are no longer necessary. Regardless of how a church conducts its services, I simply cannot comprehend the acceptance of church without the Holy Spirit. Many former Spirit-filled believers are leaving their churches in search of a culture more timed and life fitting. Have we made church more and more about us and less about Him? It is beyond my understanding and ability to worship without Spirit and truth. Yet this movement is one of the fastest growing in the land. Another movement is the inclusion message that allows congregants to recognize God in the way they see best. No longer do all teach that Jesus is the only way to the Father. No longer do we stand uncompromisingly on the Word of God. Many have compromised, and many have forfeited their spirit just like Saul. I am not looking to condemn, but one doesn't have to look far to see what I'm writing about. How can we serve Jesus without the Spirit?

How do some call themselves Christian without the representation of Christ? How can one be saved unless the Spirit draws them?

> **(John 6:44 NLT)** *"For no one can come to me unless the Father who sent me draws them to me."*

Many popular teachings are in direct contrast against the Word of God. A church not filled with His Spirit and church goers not filled with His Spirit are nothing more than an exposition, a large social gathering for display. These are difficult words for me to write but someone must declare a need for the Spirit of God to return to our churches and our lives. We must make the Davidic plea and pray, please don't take your presence. May we all retain a desperate burden for more of His presence and more of the Holy Spirit. I am anxious to see and passionate to preach the need and desire for such an outpouring that will shake the foundation of all that we know and believe. May God rest His Spirit upon us again like the great outpouring of Azusa Street.

William Booth 1829-1912, Preacher and founder of the Salvation Army said, "I consider the chief dangers which will confront the twentieth century will be; religion without the Holy Spirit, Christianity without Christ, forgiveness without regeneration, morality without God, heaven without hell."

The Price of Compromise

A compromise should never be discussed or presented that contradicts the Word of God. Why, because compromising means that one side or the other must reach an agreement to settle differences. Compromise requires the blending qualities of two things. I believe we can grow as a diverse society without compromise of the Word.

We can love and respect people and their differences, but we don't have the right to compromise His Word. Yet we are hearing such a message increasingly preached more and more. I believe some have allowed the enemy to fool them into twisting scripture to suit the seeker friendly crowd. The world has declared war against the gospel, proclaiming no more condemnation and conviction or we won't attend church. And some churches are happy to oblige. We have misunderstood conviction to be condemnation. Hearing the Word is supposed to convict. Hearing the Word is supposed to compel one to repent. After all, isn't that the point? Some new age church leaders will say conviction is too much pressure to put on a new guest. My friends, preaching the true uncompromising Word will cause you to repent, laugh, weep, forgive, love, and even pray for your enemies.

> (**2 Timothy 4:2 NLT**) *"Preach the Word. Be prepared, whether the time is favorable or not. Patiently correct, rebuke, and encourage your people with good teaching."*

Here we have clear direction with how we are to preach the Word. The Word will come with correction, rebuke, and exhortation. If you sit in a church and never hear such things, then the Word is not being preached. The Word tells us and convicts us when we are doing wrong. The Word tells us when we are living in sin. This is not to shame or hurt us. This is for us to recognize the sin and get rid of it. The Word is a guide that leads you to the loving heart of God and steers you away from sin and disobedience. Conviction and rebuke are to lead one to repentance. The Word will also bring encouragement and comfort. Hearing the truth will lead one to salvation and mold you into the likeness of Christ. What would be the point of reading the Bible and listening to sermons if what you hear and read doesn't transform you? Another common new practice is to preach sermons that make you feel like you're in a counseling session. Countless sermons are being preached and books are being written without much of a reference to the Word at all. The focus is on your feelings, your thoughts, and your attitude. Those can be good sermon's when they're preached occasionally, but a constant digestion of counsel makes one feel like they are attending psychology classes. Many Christian authors now leave out scripture to attract worldly buyers. What good is the message without the Word of the messenger? My goal here is not to discuss differences in doctrine. The intent is to review our need for the Holy Spirit and to stay true to the Word of God. My aim is to draw attention to the necessity of the breath of God. May God regenerate a thirst for His true Word.

> **(Amos 8:11 NLT)** *"The time is surely coming," says the Sovereign Lord, "when I will send a famine to the land — not a famine of bread or water but of hearing the words of the Lord."*

There are still people longing to be changed by the power of His Word. Although compromise may seem popular, there is a people longing to be transformed by the uncompromising power of the Holy Scripture. May we never become blinded and lose sight of our first love. **(Revelation 2:4 NKJV)** *"Nevertheless I have this against you, that you have left your first love."*

Thirsty Hearts

> *(Psalm 42:1-2 NKJV)* *"As the deer pants for the water brooks, so pants my soul for you, O God. My soul thirsts for God, for the living God."*

God longs for His creation to cry out and desire more of Him. Everything done and everything created was for the benefit and good pleasure of His children. I want to forget about my day, forget about all the things that trouble me, forget about the material possessions I think I need, and fall on my knees begging for more of Him. It is our gain to value His presence more than the treasures of this life. God desires that we be filled with more of Him. He desires that we would pursue Him and chase after Him as the deer panting for the water brooks. Those who truly thirst will no longer compromise and give in to the self-life. Thirsty believers will pursue His presence with a purpose like no other. **(John 3:30 NKJV)** *"He must increase, but I must decrease."* No longer can my relationship with Him be more about me. My Father desires an intimate and familiar relationship, not a drive thru hurry up and go date.

> **(Exodus 33:15 NKJV)** *"If your presence does not go up with us, do not bring us up from here."*

A.W. Tozer – The Pursuit of God "God must do everything for us. Our part is to yield and trust. We must confess and forsake the self-life then reckon it to be crucified. The cross is rough, and it is deadly, but it is effective. It does not keep its victims hanging there forever. There comes a moment when the work is finished and the suffering victim dies. After that is the resurrection glory and power, and the pain is forgotten for the joy that the veil is taken away. Lord, show us how to die, that we may rise again to newness of life."

Are you familiar with church without the Spirit? Do you know what it's like to sit through services and sermons with no anointing? How many people would honestly describe their experience as monotonous? Have you been present in the King's palace without the presence of the King? I ask these questions not to offend but to make us realize our desperate need for His presence and Spirit. There is a remedy to dead services and prayers that bear no fruit. It is simply desiring and allowing the Holy Spirit to operate as He wishes in our lives and our services. My dad taught me that if you spend the time going to church you may as well have church while you're there. He would say, "you get out of it what you put into it." No truer words have ever been spoken. So, my attempt is not to bring condemnation and make this book to seem heavy and burdensome. My purpose is to make clear our need for more of Him.

> (**Psalm 27:4 NKJV**) *"One thing have I desired of the Lord, that will I seek: that I may dwell in the house of the Lord all the days of my life, to behold the beauty of the Lord, and to inquire in His temple."*

Habitation Not Visitation

A visitation is a short temporary visit. It means that the stay won't be very long. A habitation is the act of occupying a dwelling place. The old testament saints had to settle for visitation, seeing that the Holy Spirit had not come yet. After the death of Jesus, the veil was torn granting total and unlimited access into the presence of God. Our greatest gift outside of salvation is the ability to be in constant intimate relationship with the Lord. The veil being torn leaves us with no excuses when it comes to access. We have complete access. What we do with that access is up to us. Imagine, no more dead church services and no more Spiritless prayers. No more defeated days feeling hopeless. A Spirit-filled habitation has been provided by the sacrifice of Jesus Christ.

(**Matthew 27:50–51 NKJV**) *"And Jesus cried out again with a loud voice, and yielded up His spirit. Then, behold, the veil of the temple was torn from top to bottom; and the earth quaked, and the rocks were split,"*

Anointed Spiritual Habitation

(**2 Chronicles 5:13–14 NKJV**) *"13. Indeed it came to pass, when the trumpeters and singers were as one, to make one sound to be heard in praising and thanking the Lord, and when they lifted up their voice with the trumpets and cymbals and instruments of music, and praised the Lord, saying: "For He is good, For His mercy endures forever," that the house, the house of the Lord, was filled with a cloud, so that the priests could not continue ministering because of the cloud; for the glory of the Lord filled the house of God.*

This story gives great insight about an anointed spiritual habitation. Solomon had completed the building of the temple and now it was time to bring in the furnishings and prepare for celebration. Verse 13, gives us the prerequisite for an outpouring of consuming glory. The verse tells us the musicians and singers became as one. In other words, just like on the day of Pentecost God's people were in perfect unity. Unity is a prerequisite for the presence of God.

(**Psalms 133:1, 3 NKJV**) *"Behold, how good and how pleasant it is for brethren to dwell together in unity! It is like the dew of Hermon, descending upon the mountain of Zion; for there, God commanded the blessing, life evermore."*

If God's people are to chase His presence, it must first start in unity. Then the verse goes on to detail how they made one unified sound in praising and thanking the Lord. Now we see that this unity is happening in the middle of a worship service. God recognized their unity. He recognized their praise, and the two caused Him to show up. It goes on to say the house was filled with a cloud. This cloud of course is the amazing presence of God, "Yahweh." Not only did this cloud fill the house, the presence of God was so mighty and strong that the priest could no longer minister because of the cloud. Verse 14 concludes by saying, "for the glory of the Lord filled the house of God." Wow! This is the kind of power Jesus made available to all believers. Unity and praise had caused the presence of God to be so full and present that it appeared as a cloud. Literally so thick you could cut it with a knife. But notice what the presence of God did to the priest. His supernatural presence removed human ability and caused those attending to fall prostate before His majesty. The power of God can be so strong in our lives that our earthly bodies cannot contain the glory. Good news, the story doesn't end there.

> **(2 Chronicles 6:1-2 KJV)** *Then said Solomon, The Lord hath said that he would dwell in the thick darkness. But I have built a house of habitation for thee, and a place for thy dwelling for ever.*

Solomon recognized the promise of God coming to pass just as He promised. That He would come in a thick cloud. We then see a great declaration made from Solomon. He announces the purpose of the temple was to make God a habitation, a dwelling place. The temple was not built for an unexpected visit. It was not built for the occasional drop by. It was built for God to dwell in. It was built and dedicated to God in expectation that He would abide with them forever.

> **(2 Chronicles 7:1-3 NKJV)** *When Solomon had finished praying, fire came down from heaven and consumed the burnt offering and the sacrifices; and the glory of the Lord filled the temple. And the priests could not enter the house of the Lord, because the glory of the Lord had filled the Lord's house. When all the children of Israel saw how the fire came down, and the glory of the Lord on the temple, they bowed their faces to the ground on the pavement, and worshiped and praised the Lord, saying: "For He is good, For His mercy endures forever."*

I encourage you to read chapters 5-7 of 2 Chronicles to obtain the fullness of what I'm trying to capture in a few paragraphs. The continued demonstration of God's supernatural power consuming the people and the place. We see parallels in chapters 6 and 7 regarding the fullness of His presence. Solomon had prayed this amazing prayer and immediately the presence of God came and consumed and received the offering that had been given as a sacrifice. Simultaneously the glory filled the temple again and just as strong as before, causing the priest to once again fall prostate. This story gives us a perfect image of what the power and Spirit of God can and will do. As I write this I'm smiling for two reasons. The first is that I've experienced this powerful outpouring many times. And yes, many times it has overtaken those in attendance to the point which no one could stand, and of course our agenda was out the window. The second reason I smile is thinking of those folks who would be mortified at such an experience. The words in this scripture are true, and countless people can testify of the need for more. When the people witnessed this, they began to break out in more praise to the glory of God. So, now we see this group continuing to be in unity as they now pray for the blessing of the Lord. The first glorious outpouring happened with unity and praise and the second through prayer and unity followed by praise. We also don't want to miss that they had prepared their offering. This offering represents the necessity of giving back to God what belongs to Him and recognizing Him as the giver of all good things. We can already see four keys to obtain a habitation of God's presence. The first is unity, followed by praise, offering and prayer.

> **(2 Chronicles 7:12–16 NKJV)** *Then the Lord appeared to Solomon by night, and said to him: "I have heard your prayer, and have chosen this place for Myself as a house of sacrifice. When I shut up heaven and there is no rain, or command the locusts to devour the land, or send pestilence among My people, if My people who are called by My name will humble themselves, and pray and seek My face, and turn from their wicked ways, then I will hear from heaven, and will forgive their sin and heal their land. Now My eyes will be open and My ears attentive to prayer made in this place. For now I have chosen and sanctified this house, that My name may be there forever; and My eyes and My heart will be there perpetually.*

This encounter is God responding to Solomon's prayer in which he asked, "what must we do to retain God's grace should we fall into sin?" God is allowing him to know that His people will always be able to return to His grace. God first assures Solomon that He has chosen "this place" for Himself as a house of sacrifice. There are simply no greater words to hear than God saying, "I have chosen your place as my place." This is ultimately the goal of all Spirit-filled believers and Spirit-filled churches. O that God would choose our place and our lives as a house of habitation. Most all Christians know and can quote 2 Chronicles 7:14. This is God giving an exact remedy for what His people should do when trouble comes. The roadmap could not be clearer. If we do the things detailed in verse 14, He will restore everything. God's words continue to tell Solomon that His eyes are watching, and His ears are listening to the prayers made in His place. I would like to focus briefly on the first two words of verse 16, "for now." For now, means it won't always be the case. In other words, it's temporary. These two words jump off the page and remind me to never take for granted His presence and His abiding Spirit. Even the highest of spiritual seasons come to an end. For now, I have this address and these friends. Think about that just for a moment. Those two words, for now, should compel us to plead for a continual outpouring of His presence. The season you are in at this very moment is a for now season, it won't last always. Let me remind you that His Spirit can be lost like it was with Saul. Preserve it, chase after it, beg for more, but never compromise and become content in settling for less. His presence and His Spirit are always available, we must do what's necessary to keep the cloud of His presence in our lives.

5

When God Breathes - The Son

(John 1:1–3 NKJV) *"1. In the beginning was the Word, and the Word was with God, and the Word was God. 2. He was in the beginning with God. 3. All things were made through Him, and without Him nothing was made that was made."*

"In the beginning" links Jesus, the Word, with the Genesis chapter 1 creation. The Word is Jesus Christ, the absolute, eternal expression of God. The Word of God was breathed, affirming the Word as the divine agent in creation. "The Word was God" attributes deity to the Word without defining all the Godhead, Father, Son, and Spirit as the Word. The Godhead is the triune trinity of God, three in one. John 1:3, declares Jesus the Word, "Logos," was the divine agent responsible for creation. Before the Son was born as Jesus, He existed as God the Logos Word. At birth, God the incarnate Son took on flesh becoming man yet still remaining God. In the beginning God existed as three, God Yahweh, Logos the Word, and the Holy

Spirit. After Logos became flesh God existed as three, God Yahweh, Jesus the Son, and the Holy Spirit. The fall of man required God to personally present Himself incarnate as the acceptable sacrifice to redeem and reconcile mankind to Himself. God the Word, Logos, took on flesh and became the man of Jesus, God the Son.

> **(Genesis 3:15 NLT)** *"And I will cause hostility between you and the woman, and between your offspring and her offspring. He will strike your head, and you will strike his heel."*

Scripture records two times that Satan endeavored to tempt the legitimacy of the Word. The first occasion was in Genesis 3:1-5, he tempted and questioned the integrity of the Word of God when tempting Eve. The second occasion in Matthew 4:3-7, he tempted and questioned the integrity of Jesus, the Word of God incarnate. Although Eve fell to the temptation, it's interesting to note that Jesus defeated and rejected his tempting in Matthew 4 with the inspired Word.

Jesus – the Christ, our Savior and Lord

The angel declared to Mary and Joseph that His name would be Jesus. Jesus means Jehovah is salvation. When did Jesus become Christ, Savior, and Lord? Some teach He was all three at birth, but please allow me to share my thoughts. Each title has specific meaning given at specific times. Jesus is His name, Christ, Savior, and Lord are titles.

(Matthew 1:21 NKJV) *"And she will bring forth a Son, and you shall call His name Jesus, for He will save His people from their sins."*

The title Christ means anointed one. The first mention of the Spirit descending upon Jesus was at baptism.

(Matthew 3:16 NKJV) *"When He had been baptized, Jesus came up immediately from the water; and behold, the heavens were opened to Him, and He saw the Spirit of God descending like a dove and alighting upon Him."*

Immediately following baptism Jesus became the Christ. The Spirit of God descended and sat upon Him, anointing Him for the ministry to follow. Savior means one who rescues. Jesus rescued us through being the acceptable sacrifice leading to atonement.

(Philippians 3:20 NKJV) *"For our citizenship is in heaven, from which we also eagerly wait for the Savior, the Lord Jesus Christ."* **(Acts 5:31 NKJV)** *Him God has exalted to His right hand to be Prince and Savior, to give repentance to Israel and forgiveness of sins."*

Jesus became Savior when the sin of the world was placed upon Him on the cross, granting redemption. In His sacrifice, He rescued and reconciled mankind back to God.

(2 Corinthians 5:21 NKJV) *For He made Him who knew no sin to be sin for us, that we might become the righteousness of God in Him."*

Lord is having power and authority, a ruler by position. The man Jesus died on the cross. The resurrected Jesus assumed His Lordship declaring victory over death, hell, and the grave.

> **(1 Corinthians 15:20-22 NKJV)** *20. But now Christ is risen from the dead, and has become the firstfruits of those who have fallen asleep. 21. For since by one man came death, by Man also came the resurrection of the dead. 22. For as in Adam all die, even so in Christ all shall be made alive."*

Resurrection proclaimed Him as Lord and ruler.

Receive the Holy Spirit

> **(John 20:21-22 NKJV)** *"21. So Jesus said to them again, "Peace to you! As the Father has sent Me, I also send you." 22. And when He had said this, He breathed on them, "Receive the Holy Spirt."*

For the first time the Son was breathing, and the Holy Spirit was ready to find habitation with mankind. The old created man, Adam, began with the breath of God and now the new creation begins with the breath of the Son of God. The revelation of this text will prove to be one of the most important truths to be revealed in scripture.

Resurrection night, Jesus supernaturally appeared to His disciples. They had difficulty comprehending this glorified being was in fact their Master. He had promised that He'd rise on the third day but one can understand their hesitation. Jesus showed them His hands and His side to prove He was in fact the resurrected Savior. His goal before death was to train and equip His disciples and followers to go out and witness. That did not change after the resurrection. His first commission was "As the Father sent Me, I also send you." Jesus the man fulfilled His destiny, becoming Jesus Christ our Savior and Lord. Atonement and justification came through the death and resurrection of Jesus Christ. Prior to these events, no one had ever been granted a personal reconciled relationship with God. Jesus made salvation possible. Until resurrection, the disciples followed Jesus, God in flesh. After resurrection, He appeared to them as Jesus, the Son of God in a glorified body. Salvation, justification, sanctification, and reconciliation all became available with the death and resurrection of Jesus. In John 20:22, the disciples became the first recipients of personal Holy Spirit-filled salvation through Jesus Christ. The difference in knowing Him relationally and intimately is the Holy Spirit. This text details the first encounter when believers could personally receive the Holy Spirit. When Jesus breathed, those breathed upon received salvation and the gift of atonement. The disciples had followed Him for three years, but they were never reborn or saved by the Spirit. That couldn't have been possible because the sacrifice had not yet been given. "Receive the Holy Spirit" is the act of those in attendance being born again of the Spirit.

> **(1 Corinthians 5:17 NKJV)** *"Therefore, if anyone is in Christ, he is a new creation; old things have passed away; behold, all things have become new."*

The Holy Spirit has a two-fold purpose. The first is salvation, the Spirit of life.

> **(Romans 8:2 NKJV)** *"For the law of the Spirit of life in Christ Jesus has made me free from the law of sin and death."*

When you accept Jesus as your Savior, you are receiving salvation and accepting the Spirit to abide in you. The second purpose of the Holy Spirit is to manifest in power, enabling believers for their commission. Every believer has the commission of ministry, witness, and service. The manifesting Spirit that came on Pentecost will be discussed in later chapters.

> **(Acts 1:8 NKJV)** *"But you shall receive power when the Holy Spirit has come upon you; and you shall be witnesses to Me in Jerusalem, and in all Judea and Samaria, and to the end of the earth."*

> **(Luke 24:49 NKJV)** *"Behold, I send the promise of My Father upon you; but tarry in the city until you are endued with power from on high."*

> **(Read Romans 8:11-17)** *"11But if the Spirit of Him who raised Jesus from the dead dwells in you, He who raised Christ from the dead will also give life to your mortal bodies through His Spirit who dwells in you."*

When God the Father Breathes, it gives life.
When God the Son Breathes, it brings salvation.

The Acceptable Sacrifice

(Romans 3:24-25 NKJV) *"24. Being justified freely by His grace through the redemption that is in Christ Jesus. 25. Whom God set forth as a propitiation by His blood, through faith, to demonstrate His righteousness, because*

in His forbearance God had passed over the sins that were
previously committed."

Because of Jesus we are justified, declared righteous, in the sight of God. Jesus was our propitiation, the acceptable sacrifice to redeem man. Study of Jesus Christ as the propitiation reveals that He is the shadow of the Old Testament Mercy Seat. Jesus was the only saving solution to God's wrath for sin. We are free from sin by His blood, through faith. Sin's penalty has been paid for those who are being saved now and those who lived prior to resurrection, "God had passed over the sins that were previously committed." When Jesus breathed, He secured payment for ransom, granting redemption. Man has been reconciled to God, the bond is the blood of Jesus Christ, the acceptable sacrifice.

Breathe on Me

As I said before, I have been in church since before I was born. I don't regret one minute and see no reason for change. Attending church didn't bring me salvation. Singing and playing church music didn't do it either. Both my parents are pastors but even that doesn't grant me redemption. Accepting Jesus Christ as your personal Savior is the only way to receive salvation. All details to salvation can be found in the book of Romans, called the Romans Road.

> **(Romans 10:9-10 NKJV)** *9. "That if you confess with your mouth the Lord Jesus and believe in your heart that God has raised Him from the dead, you will be saved. 10. For with the heart one believes unto righteousness, and with the mouth confession is made unto salvation."*

I personally felt the Spirit drawing me when I was twelve years old. I sat through church services for twelve years, but something was different on one particular night. As Pastor Walter had finished his sermon and the service moved into what we titled "the altar call." Never had I felt the draw of the Holy Spirit to salvation. We all stood as the altar song began. I don't remember the sermon, but I remember the song was "I just started living," and my Uncle Ricky was singing. Standing in the second row on the right side of the church, my heart started beating in an unfamiliar way. Suddenly tears began to fall down my face as the twelve-year-old boy was trying to figure out what was happening. I was standing beside of my church buddy, my cousin Joe. The next thing I knew I was weeping at the altar crying out to Jesus. Though I was young, I had a real and radical Jesus encounter. Suddenly I knew what it meant to be breathed on by the Son. My life would never be the same. That night in Logan County, West Virginia, at Orville Holiness Church, I gave my life to Jesus and received Him as my Savior. He breathed on me and I received the gift of the Holy Spirt. I wasn't always a model Christian, but I've kept the faith and His mercies are new every morning. When God the Son breathed, I received salvation in Jesus through the Holy Spirit.

6

The Gifts of the Son

The gifts of the Son are vital in assuring that the gifts of the Father and the Spirit are properly and effectively applied in the body of the church. The Son gifts are office gifts to facilitate and equip the body. Equipping the saints requires training and preparation. Without the manifestation and operation of the ministry gifts in the church, the saints will not mature, nor be equipped to do the work of the ministry. The office gifts develop believers, qualifying them for ministry and service in the body. There is a need to govern and shepherd the prophetic and the supernatural. The call to supernatural empowerment requires mentoring, impartation and discipline. Without the covering of office gifts, the supernatural would function chaotically rather than edifying the body. The five ministry offices are for nurturing and equipping His church, not for hierarchical control or ecclesiastical competition.

I can testify that the supernatural is biblical and destined for the benefit of believers. I have witnessed and participated in the power of God and the Spirit of God. The Spiritual gifts have been commonly in use all my life. Healings, miracles, the expelling of demons, I've witnessed these and more. I've also been under and served with outstanding men and woman fulfilling the offices of the five-fold ministries. If you've attended church long enough you've witnessed great leadership governed by the scripture. Unfortunately, you've probably also witnessed bad leadership, novice leadership, or rebellious leadership. The office gifts are needed in the church. Not bodies filling positions, but men and women called and anointed to serve and lead the body of Christ. The lack of anointed leadership will leave an open path to problems. Most anyone who has attended a full-gospel, Pentecostal, or Spirit-filled church has witnessed the supernatural become unnecessarily dysfunctional. This is never the fault of the Spirit. Dysfunction comes when proper training is neglected or refused. My parents and my pastors exposed me to wonderful supernatural experiences. But those experiences did not come without the display of foolish behavior. There seems to always be someone who doesn't know how to function in their gift. Others may refuse the guidance or covering of spiritual leadership. Therefore, constant training and discipleship is necessary and that's why God has established leaders to oversee the supernatural. I have received much training and equipping from my coverings, nonetheless, I was very hesitant in allowing Spiritual gifts to flow through me because of the abuse I had witnessed. I wanted nothing to do with the showoff or misusing of these gifts. I have respect for the gifts and I understood the command for order.

(1 Corinthians 14:40 NKJV) *"Let all things be done decently and in order."*

The office gifts are necessary for the training and equipping needed for proper operation of all gifts. Gifts need accountability and gifts need a spiritual covering. Anyone refusing accountability is reckless and dangerous to the church and the body. A rebellious spirit is a wicked spirit. God knew the supernatural would need protected and that His children would need to be educated how to function in the supernatural. Thus, we are given the office gifts of the five-fold ministries.

> **(Ephesians 4:11-16 NKJV)** *"11. And He Himself gave some to be apostles, some prophets, some evangelist, and some pastors and teachers, 12. for the equipping of the saints for the work of ministry, for the edifying of the body of Christ, 13. till we all come to the unity of the faith and of the knowledge of the Son of God, to a perfect man, to the measure of the stature of the fullness of Christ; 14 that we should no longer be children, tossed to and fro and carried about with every wind of doctrine, by the trickery of men, in the cunning craftiness and deceitful plotting, 15 but, speaking the truth in love, may grow up in all things into Him who is the head- Christ — 16 from whom the whole body, joined and knit together by what every joint supplies, according to the effective working by which every part does its share, causes growth of the body for the edifying of itself in love."*

Before we look at the ecclesiology of the fivefold ministry gifts, let's briefly study the purpose of these gifts. In Ephesians 4, I can find ten points setting the foundation for the necessity of these gifts. Provided are the ten purposes of the fivefold ministry.

1. For the perfecting and equipping of the saints.
2. For the work of the ministry.
3. For the edifying of the body.

4. Til we all come in the unity of faith.
5. And of the knowledge of the Son of God.
6. Unto a perfect man.
7. To the measure of the stature of the fullness of Christ.
8. Be no more children, tossed to and fro with every wind of doctrine.
9. Speaking the truth in love.
10. Recognizing Christ is the Head.

The Fivefold Office Ministry Gifts

(1) Apostle

A delegate anointed of God and appointed by the Son, given authority to act on behalf of the Lord Jesus as an ordained leader of the body. The apostle is a messenger or sent one as a spokesman. They build and oversee ministries while equipping the saints. The apostle will first preach and teach the Word, acquiring the role and call of apostle once established in the Word. However, not all preachers and teachers become apostles. The word apostle was used of those twelve disciples whom Jesus sent out to expand His ministry. These same disciples were recommissioned after the resurrection to be His witnesses throughout the world. (Read Luke 24:46–49, Acts 1:8) Later, we find others appointed as apostles such as the Apostle Paul. They were pioneers in making converts, equipping the saints and planting churches. There are views that believe apostles were confined to the first generation of Christians. Some teach that apostles do not exist today and that only those who witnessed the resurrected Jesus could be apostles. I'll let other books and teachings debate the case, but I do not believe this theory. I am personally acquainted with great men and women of God who walk in the ordained calling of apostle. Ephesians 4:11 specifically list five office ministries and they are listed as a collective group. I can find no reason why we should believe that only four of the five exist today. If so, why mention the five together. Many of the same people who argue against the modern–day apostle teach only seven spiritual gifts. They argue that the gifts of tongues and interpretation were only for the first-generation Christians. If this were the case I'd feel somewhat cheated. I find the office of apostle necessary today and beneficial to the body. I am familiar with some of the groups that argue against the office of the apostle. Many of them have overseers and church planters but they usually call them bishop or district overseer. Changing titles to fit one's doctrinal argument does not hide the need for the office of the Apostle. I agree with the teaching of classes of apostles. One class is the Apostles of the Lamb, the twelve Apostles.

(Revelation 21:14 NKJV) *"Now the wall of the city had twelve foundations, and on them were the names of the twelve apostles of the Lamb."*

The qualifications of the apostles of the Lamb are listed in Acts 1:15-22. There will never be another apostle added to this group, as they had to be present with Jesus. Another class is known as the Other Foundational Apostles. These apostles helped lay the foundation of the New Covenant doctrine. The Apostle Paul would be the most recognizable of this group. **(Ephesians 3:4-5, Ephesians 2:19-20, 1 Corinthians 3:10)** Another class is the Non-Foundational Apostles. These apostles came after the foundation was laid and continue to serve today, building on the foundation. This apostle is an ambassador sent to build up and tear down, to equip and train, and to share the uncompromised message of the gospel. This group includes modern day missionaries and pastors. Again, not all pastors and missionaries are called to be apostles, but many serve in the role of expanding the kingdom. Many also teach that modern apostles are intertwined with the role of prophet. The evidence of the apostles anointing is signs, wonders, and mighty deeds.

> **(2 Corinthians 12:12 NKJV)** *"Truly the signs of an apostle were accomplished among you with all perseverance, in signs and wonders and mighty deeds."*

A true apostle plants and establishes new works while a false apostle will divide while planting evil seeds of envy and strife.

(2) Prophet

A delegate chosen and ordained to speak on behalf of God and to communicate God's given message to the people. A prophet is called, appointed, and anointed of God, not elected by man. The prophet is called and anointed to protect, warn, watch, direct, guide, and lead. Except for God's call, prophets have no listed specific qualifications in scripture. They are called from all walks of life and all classes of society. Nor does the call apply to one certain gender. The Bible lists approximately 78 prophets and prophetesses as individuals or groups. Prophets are given messages, from the Lord, to speak directly to an individual, a nation, or a group of people such as a church or nation. Some prophets were called for a lifetime while others spoke briefly and no more. The prophet has one specific role, proclaim the word given to them by God through the Holy Spirit. Prophets equip and train through teaching and preaching, however, not all prophets are called as pastor or apostle. It is important to note that the office gift of prophet is different from that of the Spiritual gift of prophecy. Both proclaim God given messages but again, one is an office and the other a gift. Prophets do exist today, however, it is wise to test the fruit of messages received. Many Godly men and women seek to hear the voice of God while others seek to obtain a fancy exciting word. The true prophet is necessary for the perfecting and equipping of the saints.

(3) Evangelist

One who is commissioned and ordained to proclaim the gospel in preaching the Word of God uncompromisingly. The evangelist preaches and teaches to establish converts, making them disciples for Christ. Evangelist are more specifically called to go out and compel, whereas other ministries are called to shepherd and feed one flock. Though they mostly travel and witness abroad, it is wise and necessary for an evangelist to be under the covering of a house. Evangelist need to be fed and equipped just like every other office gift and believer. Some are appointed to evangelistically preach inside and outside the churches, but all Christians are called to evangelize in witnessing. The office of evangelist generally does serve as a shepherd, although some churches and organizations have intertwined the gift with that of overseers.

(4) Pastor

The feeder, protector, guide, and shepherd of God's flock. The term pastor had not become official until mentioned in Ephesians 4. Prior to that the term always meant shepherd, one who attends to the care and need of the flock. The pastor is to oversee and lead the body as directed by the scripture. Unlike the previously mentioned office gifts, the pastor is commissioned to shepherd an appointed flock. The members of the flock may change but the pastor's call remains the same. Some churches and denominations are flexible to appoint and title the five-fold ministers differently.

(5) Teacher

The supernatural ability to explain and apply the truths received from God's Word. One who instructs by imparting knowledge and information. Biblical teaching is often referred to as instruction in the faith. Thus, teaching and instructing is different from preaching, or the proclamation of the gospel to the non-Christian world. Special attention is given to the danger of false teachings. Scripture instructs us to test the messenger and the message. (Read 2 Timothy 3:1-7 & 1 Peter 2:1-3) Teachers are gifted to explain and instruct the body in the depths and mysteries of the Word. The gifts of pastor and teacher often intertwine in administration.

It is not my goal or intent to give absolute definitions or roles to the office gifts. The Scripture is thorough and altogether complete in detailing the functions to be performed. Certain roles with each office gifts are absolute, other roles may be flexible in design to fit the body and church structure in which they serve. Flexibility is allowed in reason but redefining the office gifts to better suit a situation is not permitted in Scripture. One unarguable fact is that all the office gifts are called to lead in the equipping of the saints. The call and the Spiritual equipping have to do with the transformation and development of believers. The qualifications of each role listed in Scripture have to do with the outward character and the inward Spirit. The ultimate prerequisite for each role is the call and anointing of God.

Honoring the Office

Without the proper foundation, we cannot function as we should. When the office gifts were created, the focus was the function of the office rather than the title. It's an office with a title, not a title with an office. When we honor the office, we establish the biblical foundation which allows recognition of the title.

> **(Ephesians 2:19-22 AMP)** *"19. So then you are no longer strangers and aliens [outsiders without rights of citizenship], but you are fellow citizens with the saints (God's people), and are [members] of God's household, 20 having been built on the foundation of the apostles and prophets, with Christ Jesus himself as the [chief] cornerstone, 21 in whom the whole structure is joined together, and it continues [to increase] growing into a holy temple in the Lord [a sanctuary dedicated, set apart, and sacred to the presence of the Lord]. 22 In Him [and in fellowship with one another] you also are being built together into a dwelling place of God in the Spirit."*

The functionality of the five-fold offices establish and secure the foundation. To obtain the blessing of God we must walk in and revere the office gifts. Upholding the banner of the Lord in right living and biblical reverence will bring recognition to the title. Still, the goal is not a title but to serve faithfully in the office. In doing so, the members of the body are to respect and observe the authority of those in the office gifts.

> **(Romans 13:1 NKJV)** *"Let every soul be subject to the governing authorities. For there is no authority except from God, and the authorities that exist are appointed by God."*

Respect is earned, not demanded. In honoring the God that anointed and appointed us to the office, we will earn the respect of God and the people, because the Holy Spirit will confirm the call. Authority has a divine order. One cannot usurp authority. It must be given by the Lord. The divine order is like that of the anointing oil poured on Aarons head, that passed down the beard, running to the body. Preceding this divine order is unity in the body.

> **(Psalms 133:1-3 NKJV)** *"1 Behold, how good and how pleasant it is for brethren to dwell together in unity! 2 It is like the precious oil upon the head, running down on the beard, the beard of Aaron, running down on the edge of his garments. 3 It is like the dew of Hermon, descending upon the mountains of Zion; for there the Lord commanded the blessing — Life forevermore."*

The Divine order, is that authority and vision are given to the head, those appointed and anointed to lead. Authority flows down the body, just as the oil flowed down from Aarons head to his beard, and down the garment. Jesus Christ is the head, and He appoints those in the body to fulfill the leadership roles. Those in leadership or the office gifts then equip the saints, allowing a continuous flow of the oil. Unity, along with the proper flow of oil, commands the blessing of the Lord. Authority and reverence is recognized in those called to the office gifts of the five-fold ministry, as well as the office of bishop and elder.

Prostituted Titles

All office gifts are given for the edifying and building of the body. It is unfortunate that man has prostituted titles over time to gain stature and power. If you don't know whether you are called to a five-fold ministry office, you're probably not. Equipping discipleship is necessary if you think you may have the calling but aren't sure. Submit yourself to good training under Godly leadership. The Scripture is clear regarding the body of Christ. The body has many members, yet one body. Though the body has many members, each part has its role to play. The Bible is not misguiding concerning gifts, structure, and governance of God's people. Still there are those who will self-proclaim titles to gain stature. This is unnecessary and needs corrected.

(Ephesians 4:1b NKJV) *"Walk worthy of the calling with which you were called."*

There is a need for clarity concerning office and administration gifts. We have a duty to restore proper callings, offices, and titles, undoing the denominational and popularity of misleading titles. My title is pastor. There's no reason for me to announce my ownership of the prophet title simply because I feel it will bring more attention. Nor should I consider my title to be more important than my calling. The honor of ones calling should cause them to humbly walk proud of who they are in Christ. Many churches, organizations, and lone rangers are bringing confusion to the body because we are giving titles based upon what people want to be called rather than what their calling is. Walk worthy or you could lose the blessing like Saul did. Please allow me to expel some thoughts while giving biblical truths. Scripture does not support deacons telling shepherds how to pastor. Vision is given from the top down, not from the bottom up. Prophets aren't necessarily preachers, though some are anointed to do so. Lone ranger preachers who refuse to fall under the pastoral and apostolic authority of church leadership aren't pastors. They're dangerous and rebellious preachers. Just because someone can teach or preach does not mean they are called to be a shepherd. The heart and Spirit of the one ministering will tell whether they take pride in the title or the ministry.

> **(Matthew 7:15–16 NKJV)** *"15 Beware of false prophets, who come to you in sheep's clothing, but inwardly are ravenous wolves. 16 You will know them by their fruits."*

Each office of the five-fold ministry is called and anointed to govern and train the body. Elders, bishops, and deacons are biblically to be appointed by the governing body. Although churches have changed the way we appoint and elect over time, scripture teaches theocracy and not democracy.

> **(Philippians 1:1 NIV)** *"To all God's holy people in Christ Jesus at Philippi, together with the overseers and deacons."*

The writer is directing his words to three categories of people, the saints, the overseers, and the deacons. No confusion. Titles should be recognized but honor should be sought for the privilege of appointment to the office. Honor and respect those who are called to authority. Be cautious of those seeking promotion, accolades, and titles for self-gain. A refusal for accountability is the first clue to a rogue ministry. Be cautious of those who seek the spectacular while ignoring the supernatural. There are many who are called and anointed to operate in more than one gift. There are many who can carry more than one title because of the calling and anointing God has given them. If a man or woman of God honors their God and their calling, follow them. If a man or woman honors their title, please pray and test the fruit of their ministry.

(Matthew 7:20 NKJV) *"Therefore by their fruits you will know them."*

7

Under the Anointing

The anointing is required for manifested Spiritual ministry. Jesus did not begin His ministry until He was baptized in water and in Spirit. If we learn anything from the example of Jesus' ministry, it's that we should not attempt ministry without the call and anointing of God. The anointing is absolutely necessary to have success. Why do I say this? Anything accomplished is only through and by the anointing. We are simply vessels used to get the work done. The anointing consecrates you. The anointing enables you. The anointing honors you. The anointing gives you authority. The anointing destroys bondage. The anointing imparts the truth of God's Word. The anointing causes you to understand the ways of the Lord.

> **(Luke 4:17-21 NKJV)** *"17 And He was handed the book of the prophet Isaiah. And when he had opened the book, He found the place where it was written: 18 The Spirit of the Lord is upon me, because He has anointed Me to preach the gospel to the poor; He has sent me to heal the*

brokenhearted, to proclaim liberty to the captives and recovery of sight to the blind, to set at liberty those who are oppressed; 19 to proclaim the acceptable year of the Lord. Then He closed the book, and gave it back to the attendant and sat down. And the eyes of all who were in the synagogue were fixed on Him. 21 And He began to say to them, today this scripture is fulfilled in your hearing."

Jesus selected Isaiah 61 to launch His ministry and to announce that He was the Messiah. The anointing is the evidence of the Spirit of the Lord, God on and in flesh, doing things beyond the abilities of flesh. It is God manifesting His power on, in and through earthen vessels. To be under the anointing is to be under the covering of the Holy Spirit, empowered by Him to perform supernatural works. The anointing is evidence of Holy Spirit power. Think of the last time you witnessed someone preaching and suddenly a shift occurs with evidence of Holy Ghost power. You no longer focus on the messenger but the anointing. It's as if you would cover that person with a big blanket, to cover them so they are not visible yet continuing to minister. You don't see them, you see what's on them, a supernatural covering. The evidence of the Holy Spirit has empowered and anointed them beyond human capability.

Jesus proclaimed His ministry would be that necessary of the coming Messiah. Focusing on the down and out, the unsaved, the poor in spirit and the brokenhearted. Ultimately freeing captives under sins hold. Isaiah 61, describes the deliverance of exiled Israel in terms of the year of Jubilee. The final fulfillment was to be the coming of the Messianic Age. Jesus unwaveringly announces He is the promised Messiah. He finished His reveal by telling them, "today this scripture is fulfilled." Now that He was water baptized,

Holy Spirit baptized and under the anointing, it was time to start His ministry. Even Jesus needed to be breathed upon by the Holy Spirit. My friend, make no mistake of the importance of the Holy Spirit. If the Son of God required it, we require it too. Powerful, life changing ministry cannot happen without the empowerment of the Spirit of God.

> **(Acts 10:38 NKJV)** *"How God anointed Jesus of Nazareth with the Holy Spirit and with power, who went about doing good and healing all who were oppressed by the devil, for God was with Him."*

The Holy Spirit reveals Himself in power. Enabling human vessels to do supernatural things beyond human capability. God anointed and appointed Jesus. He is the Christ, the anointed one. The anointing allows the believer to flow in the Spiritual gifts and have authority over satan. We have absolute power and authority over the enemy through the anointing of the Holy Spirit. This power does not come from within mankind randomly. It comes from the Anointed One, Christ. Each time Jesus sent out His disciples He commanded them to operate in gifts and take authority over spirits and oppression. This is only possible by those who are anointed and called.

> **(Ephesians 3:19-20 NKJV)** *"19 to know the love of Christ which passes knowledge; that you may be filled with all the fullness of God. 20 Now to Him who is able to do exceedingly abundantly above all that we can ask or think, according to the power that works in us."*

Do not overlook or neglect the need to be filled with all the fullness of God. All Christians need to be full, complete, abundant and lacking nothing. Most everyone has heard verse 20 quoted at some point. But many times, the messenger stops at telling us that God can do anything and that nothing is beyond His ability. But that's not exactly what it says. God can do anything, but in our lives and ministries He completes the work according to the anointing in and on the believer. Notice the last line, "according to the power that works in us." My miracle, my ministry, the signs and wonders that could be following me are dependent upon the anointing and power that operates in me. He can accomplish anything but what happens through me will depend on the level of anointing on me.

> **(1 John 2:20, 27a NKJV)** *"20 But you have an anointing from the Holy One, and you know all things. 27a But the anointing which you have received from Him abides in you,"*

Christians possess an understanding of spiritual realities, guided by the Holy Spirit. The anointing will divide truth from error. The anointing provides knowledge beyond human intellect.

> **(Isaiah 10:27 KJV)** *"And it shall come to pass in that day, that his burden shall be taken away from off thy shoulder, and his yoke from off thy neck, and the yoke shall be destroyed because of the anointing."*

This anointing spoke of Gods promise to once again raise up consecrated men and women, anointed of God for the ministry. In the Old Testament, kings, priests and prophets were anointed with oil before being appointed to their office. Example of this oil anointing would be David and Aaron. In the New Testament, the Holy Spirit is poured upon those consecrated. The anointing destroys the yoke, removing the burden of bondage from God's people. It's important to notice the word destroy. The text says the yoke would be destroyed because of the anointing. To destroy something is to cause it to no longer exist, to defeat and totally demolish. The power of the anointing annihilates and extinguishes the burden. Only the supernatural power of God can do such a thing.

Protect the Anointing

Your anointing is a precious gift. More valuable than any material gain offered by this world. The anointing's worth is priceless, which is why the enemy continuously attacks yours. When you have the anointing, you must protect it. Protect the anointing of your position and calling by walking worthy of your vocation. Protect the anointing of your gifts by staying pure, holy and consecrated for the work of the Lord. The enemy gains victory any time one's anointing is compromised or diminished. You worked hard in overcoming to get what you have. Always be mindful that your anointing can decrease as well as increase. Protect your anointing as the most valuable asset you have.

(Psalm 105:15 NKJV) *"Do not touch My anointed ones, and do My prophets no harm."*

God takes it very personal when His anointing is abused or misused. He will protect His anointed, provide for His anointed and defend His anointed. Those who carry great anointing are the generals of the faith. They not only carry great responsibility, they represent the Anointed One. The anointed have the promise, "I will never leave thee not forsake thee." Righteous living sacrifices will continually grow in the anointing. Self-center disobedience will cause one to lose their anointing. Some argue the anointing cannot be lost but I would refer you to our earlier story of Saul losing God's blessing. The anointing can be lost, more appropriately, forfeited. Sometimes the anointed abuse the anointing. Other times the enemy attacks your anointing, attempting to stop your assignment. We abuse our anointing when we do not conduct ourselves according to His will.

(1 John 2:6 NKJV) *"He who says he abides in Him ought himself also to walk just as He walked."*

The enemy will attack your anointing through any means necessary. He cannot attack your anointing directly, so he does it through attacking the person whom the anointing is on. Have you ever heard it said; don't allow just anyone to touch you? Don't allow just anyone to pray for you. Don't attend every church you're invited to attend. These are statements you'll hear anointed people say. I am of the group to believe we should take caution in who prays over us, what churches we attend, and who we allow to be in our inner circle. Some say the gift of the anointing is from God and doesn't belong to you. Only God gives it and only God can take it away. This may be true, but the attack is not on your anointing. The goal of an attack is to kill, steal and destroy the one possessing the anointing. Yes, satan would like to take you out. But honestly, he's more interested in what you contain. Again, this is accomplished by attacking the person, not the presence of God on a person.

I would caution you to not allow everyone to pray over you. Not everyone who prays has good intentions. Not everyone who seeks to pray for others are anointed to do so. Not everyone in church carries the Spirit of God. I would caution you to not accept every invitation to minister. When I was young and zealous I accepted every invitation to preach. Over time I grew in God, learning that I was not to preach in every church. I am not assigned to every house who calls. These are times when we need to rely on the gift of discerning of spirits. Not every smile in church is holy, nor is every person attending church. There are dangerous people and dangerous spirits working through people who attend church and even carry titles. Some of my most evil encounters came from people who carry high esteemed titles. So yes, I would caution you to be careful. I've also witnessed great anointed ministries suffer ministry ending damage from involvement in things they were not called to. I personally know pastors who lost the anointing through disobedience while others lost it by falling into sin. Some stay in places they were not called to while others followed titles rather than anointing. God will anoint you for His purpose, not for your purpose. The Israelites lost God's promise to murmuring complaints in disobedience. They died in the wilderness. Stay in your lane and seek the Lord's will. Thankfully, many who lose the anointing recognize the loss before it's too late and they seek restoration. The calling on your life is irrevocable; the anointing with evidence is not.

(Romans 11:29 NKJV) *"For the gifts and the calling of God are irrevocable."*

Once you have been called and ordained, once you've been given spiritual gifts, they are yours for life. But you can lose the power to function in those callings and gifts. Without the power, there are no signs. Without the anointing, there is no evidence of the Holy Spirit.

Ministry without the Holy Spirit is lifeless ministry. I implore you to make sure your gifts and callings are covered by the anointing. Many people will attempt to influence in their gifts and callings without the covering of the Holy Spirit. Blinded by the illusion of success without the Spirit. Blinded of the knowledge they walk alone. Precious is the sweet anointing of God. Precious are His gifts, His callings and His presence. One guard against wrongly using your gift is to have a Godly covering with accountability. A rebellious spirit is quickly recognized in those who refuse covering and accountability. Vigorously will I protect Him. Vigorously will I protect Him on me. Vigorously will I protect Him in me. To be under the anointing is to be under the protective shadow of the Almighty. Guard what has been given to you.

(1 Timothy 6:20 NLT) *"Guard what God has entrusted to you."*

It's not uncommon for me to receive requests to preach in other churches or events. I honestly enjoy the opportunity to share outside of our church. It's also not uncommon for any one of our pastors to travel elsewhere. We once received an invitation that seemed odd from the start. The invite came from a church several hours away. We did not know the pastor or the church but one of our staff employees was friends with a member of this church. He frequently esteemed our pastoral staff's abilities to teach and preach when he was with this friend. The invitation was for any of our pastors to come do a half week revival. Needless to say, I thought it odd that an unfamiliar church would call and ask for any one of our pastors to come. I trust all our pastors, otherwise they would not be one of our pastors. I also know that not every preacher or teacher can minister in every church. I've been preaching long enough to know that my style of preaching would not be suitable for every congregation. I inquired to get some information about the makeup of this inviting church. After some prayer and dialog, I decided it would be best to provide one of our teaching pastors. I picked the pastor and he eagerly accepted. This revival would require him to stay out of town for a couple days, but all details were resolved and everything was set. At least we thought. The inviting pastor had scheduled the revival to be held Wednesday through Saturday, a total of four nights. A couple of weeks later we received a call from that pastor stating that the dates needed to be changed because his deacons didn't approve of the Wednesday through Saturday. They informed the pastor that the only way they would agree to let him hold revival was if he held it Sunday through Wednesday. I didn't mind the change of dates. I did mind sending one of our pastors into a situation where the pastor of that church did not have freedom. This church was not functioning biblically sound. It was not a healthy church. The pastor did not have the ability to seek vision nor hear from God. He was bound by a group of deacons usurping their unbiblical authority. When the pastor is bound, the church is bound. I now felt that sending our selected pastor would prove to be unhealthy. He and I agreed that due to this unhealthy structure, he would not get much accomplished by teaching in this church. If the gospel is unproductive due to unhealthy structure, you must protect your anointing. The inviting pastor gave us an out because of the changes and so we took it. We did not have to say anything. Unfortunately, that pastor held most of the disappointment. He nonchalantly shared his grief with his board and indicated that he would most likely not move forward with a revival at all. I cannot say it enough, protect your anointing. Otherwise, you could end up like this pastor having no freedom and being bound.

What if I told you Jesus did not allow everyone to touch Him, nor did He want everyone touching Him. The disciples not only followed Him, they also protected Him. They protected Him from physical attacks. They protected Him from people touching Him. Protect your anointing, whatever it takes. It may surprise you to know that Jesus did not talk to everyone who talked to Him. He talked in parables so religious leaders and rebellious traditionalist wouldn't understand what He was saying.

> **(Luke 8:45–46NKJV) with emphasis** *"45 Who touched me? 46 But Jesus said, somebody touched Me, for I perceived power going out from me."*

Jesus clearly did not want just anyone touching Him. I believe He asked His disciples this question because they were supposed to be watchful of people touching Him. Why would that be important? Because every time someone touched Him power was released. Every time a need contacts your anointing, power is released. I am most lethargic after services or encounters where my anointing has been poured out. It can be exhausting to pour out the power of your anointing on others. This text tells me that Jesus had specific intentions when it came to giving out His anointing. He did not intend for everyone to extract virtue from Him. He was not interested in allowing His anointing to be abused or misused. When anointing is relinquished, it must be built back up. Please understand, the presence and anointing of God does not change. It is the capacity of the anointing the believer can contain that must be replenished. Remember from previous chapters, Scripture tells us to be continuously refilled. There is a reason we need to be replenished because we can only contain so much. So, if the human body can only contain so much, the more reason to protect what you have. If the Anointed One saw need to protect it, then we should as well.

Have you ever witnessed or viewed a service where someone was operating strongly in the anointing, maybe praying for the sick or speaking prophetically? Many times, that movement will end abruptly, without notice. This happens for one of three reasons. The first is that the Holy Spirit declares an end to the work. The second reason is that the person under the anointing has relinquished there anointing and there's no more to pour out. The third is that the human body requires rest after carrying and giving great anointing. Mark 4:35-40, tells of Jesus requesting to cross the river to get to the other side. It says that, "He left the crowd behind," and when He got in the boat He immediately fell asleep. Jesus Himself set boundaries on His time and his anointing. Jesus sees that there is work to be done. He sees the crowd. He knows that people need healed and spirits and devils need cast out, yet He still tells His disciples to get in the boat. He was willing and wise in stopping when it was time to stop. He was the only one of the group mentioned to need immediate rest. So exhaustively tired it required a storm and nervously screaming disciples to wake Him. He was protecting the anointing and protecting the vessel carrying the anointing. Scripture often tells us that Jesus got away from the ministry to be ministered to.

Anointed Impartation

Old Testament kings, priest and prophets were anointed with oil. The ordination of said offices would require those already serving in these positions to pour oil over them, consecrating them for the office. Again, refer to David being anointed by Samuel and the anointing of Aaron. This was no longer required after the Holy Spirit came. In the New Testament, the Holy Spirit covers and baptizes you, essentially anointing you. Our anointing comes from the Holy Spirit. This amplifies the question, why are elders told to anoint other believers with oil?

> **(James 5:13-14 NKJV)** *"13 Is anyone among you suffering? Let him pray. Is anyone cheerful? Let him sing psalms. 14 Is anyone among you sick? Let him call for the elders of the church, and let them pray over him, anointing him with oil in the name of the Lord."*

This text gives very clear and precise directions. If you're suffering, pray. If you're happy, sing. If you're sick, be anointed with oil by the ordained elders of the church. Why do we need to anoint with oil? Notice, it was the elders or pastors who are commissioned to do the anointing. Who are elders and pastors? They are the anointed overseers of the church, working on behalf of the Holy Spirit. Not all believers carry the anointing. Not all believers have the nine spiritual gifts. This text is revealing the necessity of transfer. Generally, those seeking this oil anointing prayer of faith do not have the same anointing as the elders. They are asking for an impartation of the Holy Spirit to activate the gifts. The elders anointed and the Spirit baptized acting as a conduit. Their anointing and gifts are imparted to the ones being anointed with oil. The oil is to symbolize the Holy Spirit, used for a point of contact to transfer Holy Spirit gifts of healing to the ones being anointed with oil by the anointed. The oil is also symbolic to the consecration of the sick and to bring healing through the faith and gifts of the elders. This prayer of faith refers to the gift of faith. This is not to say that other believers do not operate in the gifts or have the anointing. The elders are to lead, guide, protect, and shepherd the people. A genuine ordained elder will carry great anointing and flow in multiple gifts. Take note that the text uses elders as plural. Not all elders and leaders have the same gifts and not all carry the same anointing. The anointing flows through many people in different ways. As we study the gifts we learn there are diversities of gifts with different functions and actions, but the same Spirit. I believe the body of Christ has innumerable people who can anoint others with oil and pray the prayer of faith. Our church has tremendously anointed men and women who do not necessarily walk in the office of an elder, but they are greatly anointed. However, I do believe those who participate in these prayers need to be under the authority and training of the house elders, acting as liaisons. I believe anyone laying hands on others should be under the training and discipleship of the church they attend. The prerequisite of course is to be baptized in the Spirit with evidence.

> **(Mark 6:13 NKJV)** *"And they cast out many demons, and anointed with oil many who were sick, and healed them."*

8

When God Breathes - The Holy Spirit

The Holy Spirit is the expressed power and presence of God on earth; God Himself manifested in Spirit. He is the third person of the triune trinity of God. Earth's most powerful force is the promised gift of the Holy Spirit. He is omnipotent; all powerful. He is omnipresent, universal and everywhere at all times. The Holy Spirit is the fulfillment of God's promise, "I'll never leave you nor forsake you."

> **(John 14:15-18 NKJV)** *"If you love Me, keep My commandments. And I will pray the Father, and He will give you another Helper, that He may abide with you forever— the Spirit of truth, whom the world cannot receive, because it neither sees Him nor knows Him; but you know Him, for He dwells with you and will be in you. I will not leave you orphans; I will come to you".*

For those who believe, He will dwell with you and be in you. This is the promise of habitation. As long as you have the Holy Spirit you are never abandoned or orphaned. The key is to receive Him and invite Him into your life.

> **(John 14:22-26 NKJV)** *Judas (not Iscariot) said to Him, "Lord, how is it that You will manifest Yourself to us, and not to the world?" Jesus answered and said to him, "If anyone loves Me, he will keep My word; and My Father will love him, and We will come to him and make Our home with him. He who does not love Me does not keep My words; and the word which you hear is not Mine but the Father's who sent Me. "These things I have spoken to you while being present with you. But the Helper, the Holy Spirit, whom the Father will send in My name, He will teach you all things, and bring to your remembrance all things that I said to you."*

The question leading us to revelation is, "how will you manifest yourself?" Jesus did not answer in the expected individualized singular form. He answered as the representative for the Godhead. Notice His response, "We will come and make our home." Again, He is establishing the truth within the promise. He attempts to bring comfort to the hearers by delicately announcing the Holy Spirit as the Helper. He, the Helper, will teach you all that you need to know, and He will bring back to your remembrance all that I've taught you. This is Jesus' way of telling them there's nothing to worry about. Being in the presence of one member of the Godhead is being in the presence of the Godhead. They are three in one.

Holy Spirit Dispensation

Jesus taught that you were receiving and inviting the Holy Spirit into your life at salvation. The Holy Spirit seals and authenticates the receiving of redemption.

> **(Ephesians 4:30 NKJV)** *"And do not grieve the Holy Spirit of God, by whom you were sealed for the day of redemption."*

Not only does the Holy Spirit guarantee the assurance of salvation, scripture teaches that we can increase our allotment of the Holy Spirit.

> **(Ephesians 5:18 NKJV)** *"And do not be drunk with wine, in which is dispensation; but be filled with the Spirit."*

Through study we find the text to mean that one is to be continually filled, a repeated process. Once you accept Jesus and receive the Holy Spirit you can increase the measure and quantity. Scripture teaches that you can receive the Holy Spirit in fullness. You can be filled, baptized or submersed; completely given to and saturated with the Godhead. So, where does one start who wishes to receive the Holy Spirit?

> **(Acts 2:38-39 NKJV)** *"38 Repent, and let every one of you be baptized in the name of Jesus Christ for the remission of sins; and you shall receive the gift of the Holy Spirit. 39 For the promise is to you and to your children."*

The first thing you must do is repent. Accept Jesus as your Savior, confess your sins and turn away from the old way. Publicly profess your new faith in water baptism, going down into the water to bury the old and raise to new life. Doing this grants you the gift of the Holy Spirit and it is free to all who accept Jesus. Once you've received the Holy Spirit, the above Scripture teaches and encourages you to ask for more. You can be continually filled again and again, more and more, from glory to glory. A true encounter will never allow you to be satisfied with the minimal portion available. Never become satisfied, always ask for more.

The Holy Spirit's Manifestation

Spiritual personification is known when you emulate His character and His gifts. To identify as a recipient of the Holy Spirit means you will conform to His likeness and character.

> **(Galatians 5:22-23 NKJV)** *"22 But the fruit of the Spirit is love, joy, peace, longsuffering, kindness, goodness, faithfulness, 23 gentleness, self-control. Against such there is no law."*

This is known as the fruit of the Spirit, or the Holy Spirit's character. The fruit you bear must match that of the Spirit, becoming your identity. If you read the preceding verses, Galatians 5:19-21, you find the works of the flesh. An evaluation is required to determine which list you identify with. Anyone filled with the Spirit will walk in the likeness of the fruit of the Spirit. His gifts also tell of His character and presence. The Holy Spirit is also manifested in the before mentioned spiritual gifts. If you have His character, and if you operate in His gifts, you are a representative of the Godhead.

They Were Filled with the Holy Spirit

The etymology of Pentecost comes from the Greek (Pentekoste) meaning fiftieth and refers to the festival celebrated on the fiftieth day after Passover, also known as the "Feast of Weeks." The festival, or feast, of Pentecost is always seven weeks, 50 days after Easter. This feast and celebration took place long before mentioned in Acts 2. It was redefined in the birth of the New Covenant church. Easter has no fixed date which makes Pentecost a moveable feast. Passover is the celebration of God passing over the Israelites in Egypt, saving them from death. When God saw the blood on the doorpost, He passed by leaving those covered by the blood safe.

> **(Exodus 12:13 NKJV)** *"Now the blood shall be a sign for you on the houses where you are. And when I see the blood, I will pass over you; and the plague shall not be on you to destroy you when I strike the land of Egypt."*

The death of Jesus taking place during the celebration of Passover was no accident. The outpouring of the Holy Spirit on Pentecost was also no coincidence. God knows the end from the beginning. The Passover was a shadow of the coming Christ, the ultimate sacrifice. The blood of Jesus redeems us from the curse of death just as the blood of the lamb saved God's people from death in Egypt.

> **(Romans 5:8-9 NKJV)** *"8 But God demonstrates His own love toward us, in that while we were still sinners, Christ died for us. 9 Much more then, having now been justified by His blood, we shall be saved from the wrath through Him."*

The blood of the Old Testament lamb saved the people from death. The blood of the New Covenant risen lamb redeems and saves all from death.

> **(Acts 2:1-4 NKJV)** *"When the Day of Pentecost had fully come, they were all with one accord in one place. And suddenly there came a sound from heaven, as of a rushing mighty wind, and it filled the whole house where they were sitting. Then there appeared to them divided tongues, as of fire, and one sat upon each of them. ⁴ And they were all filled with the Holy Spirit and began to speak with other tongues, as the Spirit gave them utterance."*

Once again, we see the prerequisite of unity fulfilled, allowing God to move as He pleases. 120 men and women surrendered to the will of Jesus. The promise of their obedience was baptism, a submersion like never before.

> **(Acts 1:5 NKJV)** *"for John truly baptized with water, but you shall be baptized with the Holy Spirit not many days from now."*

The introduction of this baptism came in sound. The sound was that of a strong, powerful, supernatural wind. With no real idea of what to expect, the sound of mighty wind filled the house where the 120 were assembled. The sound of wind was accompanied with the supernatural spiritual gift of tongues. In an instant, they were baptized with the Holy Spirit, with evidence of divided tongues. The Holy Spirit sat on each of them as of fire, not a literal fire but the promised power, dunamis, of Spirit. I imagine this to be much like the burning bush used by God to reveal Himself and speak to Moses. The fire sat upon the bush but did not consume the bush.

(Matthew 3:11b NLT) *"He will baptize you with the Holy Spirit and with fire."*

This text also refers to divided tongues and other tongues. They spoke in a tongue familiar to those standing by, although foreign to the 120 speaking, and they spoke in the heavenly language simultaneously. The grandeur of this day and this event propelled the church into its birth.

What was the sound of the mighty rushing wind? What was this unseen display of His presence, power, and authority? Like the fire, the wind was not literal. The sound of this mighty rushing wind filled the room. Biblically, the word wind is closely linked to breathe and the Spirit. In Genesis 1, the earth was void and dark until God breathed. The spoken Logos Word channeled through the breath of God created all things. Genesis chapter 2 gives us the account of man's creation, lifeless until God breathed. We've also studied Jesus breathing on His disciples, giving them the gift of the Holy Spirit. I want to review the account of Ezekiel 37. Ezekiel had prophesied, and dry bones become bodies. Again, lifeless until God calls on the wind to breathe. The wind was the breath of God breathing life into a great exceeding army. The supernatural sound of wind on the day of Pentecost is God the Holy Spirit breathing. The Holy Spirit breathed, bringing manifested power upon the recipients. This sound of wind was the breath of God from the third person of the trinity. The Holy Spirit filled the room and instantly baptized those in attendance. Baptism covers you, all of you. When God the Son, Jesus breathes, you are filled. When the Holy Spirit breathes, you are refilled and baptized, completely covered in the anointed power of God. Baptism of the Holy Spirit is required to receive all the fullness of the power of God. Holy Spirit baptism will bring about the manifested gifts, empowering you for ministry. The Holy Spirit will fill you, cover you, functioning in and through you.

> **(Acts 1:8a NLT)** *"But you will receive power when the Holy Spirit comes upon you."*

Power comes when you are baptized, not necessarily filled. To receive this manifested power, you must pray and seek to be baptized in the Holy Spirit. You will receive the evidence of His presence and begin to operate in spiritual gifts, including divers kinds of tongues as proof of His presence.

> **(John 3:8 NLT)** *"The wind blows wherever it wants. Just as you can hear the wind but can't tell where it comes from or where it is going, so you can't explain how people are born of the Spirit."*

When God the Father breathes, it brings life.
When God the Son breathes, it brings salvation.
When God the Holy Spirit breathes, it brings power.

9

The Gifts of the Holy Spirit

The gifts of the Spirit display the manifested power and presence of the Holy Spirit and are granted to believers for the profit of the body. The gifts are not earned but are given freely to the willing, available, and obedient children of God. Spiritual gifts enable supernatural abilities, visible evidence of the divine Godhead. These gifts are distributed as the Spirit wills for edification. Spiritual gifts operate in spiritual Christians. These gifts cannot function without the presence of the Holy Spirit. False operation of the gifts without the presence of the Holy Spirit are dangerous and cheap imitations. The gifts are spiritual gifts and must have the Holy Spirit present to manifest.

> **(1 Corinthians 12:4-7 NKJV)** *"There are diversities of gifts, but the same Spirit. There are differences of ministries, but the same Lord. ⁶ And there are diversities of activities, but it is the same God who works all in all. ⁷ But the manifestation of the Spirit is given to each one for the profit of all:"*

This text gives recognition to the Godhead as facilitators; Spirit, Lord, and God. There is no set way or prediction as to how the gifts will manifest. There are nine spiritual gifts, each distinct and diverse. The gifts will be operational in various ministries and diverse in activities. We need to be educated about the gifts; know what they are and why they are given to us. Clearly, we are not to limit or set boundaries on how the Spirit will manifest through the gifts. Incontestably understanding there are diversities in gifts and ministries with varieties of activities. Allow the Spirit to have freedom and operate willingly.

> **(1 Corinthians 12:8-11 NKJV)** *"For to one is given by the Spirit the word of wisdom; to another the word of knowledge by the same Spirit; ⁹ To another faith by the same Spirit; to another the gifts of healing by the same Spirit, To another the working of miracles; to another prophecy; to another discerning of spirits; to another divers kinds of tongues; to another the interpretation of tongues: But all these worketh that one and the selfsame Spirit, dividing to every man severally as He will."*

The Nine Spiritual Gifts of the Holy Spirit:

1. Word of Wisdom
2. Word of Knowledge
3. Faith
4. Gifts of Healing
5. Working of Miracles
6. Prophecy
7. Discerning of spirits

8. Divers kinds of Tongues
9. Interpretation of Tongues

1. Word of Wisdom

The Word of Wisdom is the supernatural revelation of the divine purpose of God given by the Holy Spirit. The Spirit imparts a word to the messenger. The messenger then verbally gives that word to the recipient. This is a verbal word gift, not ordinary wisdom. The message must demonstrate that which is unborn or reveal something not yet come to pass, the future. As well, it must speak of the hidden things not normally or naturally known. The impartation, or the word, comes to the messenger through an audible voice or spiritual inspiration. The messenger will generally receive a discernable word in their Spirit along with the revelation of who the recipient is. The revelatory word can also be given through dreams or visions. A word of wisdom can be for an individual or a group. The Holy Spirit unveils the word of wisdom in the way and time He sees fit. The word of wisdom is closely linked with the gift of prophecy and the word of knowledge.

2. Word of Knowledge

The Word of Knowledge is the supernatural revelation of things known, related to present or past fact. It deals with that which exists and is already known to the recipient. This supernatural knowledge must be a word concerning something that could not be known by the one delivering the message. This gift gives supernatural insight or understanding of circumstances without assistance of human resources. This gift is also a word gift and must come in verbal message form. This verbal word is received and delivered like the word of wisdom and prophecy.

3. Faith

To derive this gift, you must study scripture to learn there are different types and levels of faith. There is natural or simple faith, saving faith, and mountain moving faith. Everyone has what is referred to as natural or simple faith. Example, you have faith that what goes up must come down.

> **(Romans 12:3b NKJV)** *"God has dealt to each one a measure of faith."*

Everyone has a basic measure of faith. The spiritual gift of faith is more than the basic measure. This faith is God's bringing to pass a supernatural change and believing for what is impossible through human instruments. The normal or natural faith believes in simple things. The gift of faith believes in moving and accomplishing the impossible. Faith is to believe with certainty without doubt.

> **(Hebrews 11:1 NKJV)** *"Now faith is the substance of things hoped for, the evidence of things not seen."*

Faith is the substance or matter of your hope, the proof of seeing that which cannot be seen. It's believing in what's unbelievable. How do you get more than the basic measure of faith?

> **(Romans 10:17 NKJV)** *"So then faith comes by hearing, and hearing the word of God."*

Faith grows with a healthy digestion of the Word. Reading the Word, studying the Word, brings growth to your faith. Every sermon you hear, and every teaching you attend, brings growth to your faith. The more Word you absorb the greater your faith becomes. Faith only grows when your intake of the Word grows. Faith can increase no other way. The greater the knowledge and reception of the Word, the greater your faith.

4. Gifts of Healing

The gifts of healing is the supernatural healing of the body, soul, and spirit. That is why the gifts of healing are plural. The Godhead is a trinity. Mankind, created in likeness, is also a trinity, therefore, healing is needed for the full trinity being of mankind and not just physical.

(1 Thessalonians 5:23 NASB) *"Now may the God of peace Himself sanctify you entirely; and make your spirit and soul and body be preserved complete, without blame at the coming of our Lord Jesus Christ."*

The body of man is made up of physical material; can be seen and touched, using the physical senses. Man was also created partly ethereal and intangible. The ethereal includes the soul, spirit, intellect, will and conscience. The ethereal characteristics of man exist beyond this life. They are eternal. The physical body is the container of the ethereal soul and spirit. Therefore, healing is needed in multiple areas in one's life; not just physical. The gifts of healing is to have the supernatural ability to pray one free from sickness, disease, oppression, brokenness, etc. Healing can take place in the physical body, the spiritual, the mind, satanic oppression and the emotion. The gifts of healing are many. The gifts are diverse and often function completely different and separate from one gift to another. Multiple people may have the gifts, while one may be for the physical, another the soul and another the spirit. Healing comes through the anointed and obedient individual when they pray for or speak healing over the recipient. Jesus commonly told His disciples to heal the sick when He sent them out. Healing took place through speaking the Word of God over the one needing healing, anointing one with oil, praying in faith, laying on of hands and even the use of handkerchiefs. Jesus never prayed asking or begging for healing, He spoke the Word as completed, "be healed." He never instructed His disciples to beg for healing. He said go and heal them. For the gifts of healing to operate there must be faith. One must be in the Spirit, and one must be called and anointed with the gifts.

> **(Isaiah 53:4–5 NKJV)** *"4 Surely He has borne our griefs and carried our sorrows; Yet we esteemed Him stricken, smitten by God, and afflicted. 5 But He was wounded for our transgressions, He was bruised for our iniquities; the chastisement for our peace was upon Him, and by His stripes we are healed."*

This text gives us the declaration of healing through the stripes Jesus bore on His body. Healing is a complete work; finished and final; "we are healed." We need not ask Him to do something He's already done. The healing of griefs and sorrows are for the emotion and soul of man. He healed our transgressions, our violations of the law, our sins. He healed our iniquities and our immorally corrupt wicked sins. The cost of our gained peace was laid upon His body; no more in bondage. The study of the given text reveals healing needed and granted in multiple areas of one's life. The Gifts of Healing are for the body, soul and spirit.

5. Working of Miracles

The working of miracles is a supernatural act accomplished by the divine power and authority of the Holy Spirit. A miracle is an occurrence that is beyond natural comprehension and must mean the laws of nature are suspended. Miracles are not possible through human channels alone and, therefore, they can only happen supernaturally by the Holy Spirit. Miracles can occur without the assistance of man but the gift of the working of miracles requires a submitted Spirit-filled believer. The Holy Spirit works through the believer to bring about the supernatural phenomenon. The miracle happens by the power of the Holy Spirit. The individual is used to bring to pass the desired outcome of the Holy Spirit. It goes without saying that those who have been granted this gift must be in total obedience to witness a miracle come to pass. Miracles should not surprise us. They are granted to be as normal and common as the other gifts.

6. Prophecy

The gift of Prophecy has three specific purposes; edification, exhortation and comfort.

(1 Corinthians 14:3 NKJV) *"But he who prophesies speaks edification and exhortation and comfort to men."*

The Scripture leaves no room for confusion. There is no other purpose to prophecy. This gift of prophecy will always bring encouragement and comfort to those who receive the message. A word given that does not edify is not this gift of prophecy. Prophecy is the anointed speaking of a word from God through the Holy Spirit. The operation and function of this gift operates like that of the Word of Wisdom and Knowledge. Those gifted with prophecy are not necessarily prophets. Prophecy is a gift and the prophet is an office.

7. Discerning of spirits

The discerning of spirits is the divine ability to identify the presence and activity of the spirit within a person, place, or event. It is a realm which the five physical senses cannot enter. Discerning of spirits produces security against false teachers, false doctrine, lies and all spiritual things of light and darkness. This gift also allows one to identify the good and right Spirit within other believers. Discerning allows you to distinguish the spirits that operate within other people or the spirits operating in places. This gift enables spiritual insight and revelation of plans and purposes of the enemy and his forces. Discerning of spirits is not the gift of suspicion. The Holy Spirit within you will identify the spirit or spirits in places and people. The discerning of spirits leaves nothing hidden; reveals what cannot be seen. This discerning of spirits is plural, allowing for the identification of all unfamiliar and dark spirits, as well as the good and righteous. Discerning of spirits not only reveals the hidden darkness, it reveals the glory in the righteous followers of God.

8. Diverse Kinds of Tongues

Diverse kinds of tongues are a vocal supernatural utterance spoken through the believer by the empowering of the Holy Spirit.

This special gift was birthed in the church on the Day of Pentecost as recorded in Acts 2. Divers kinds of tongues allows the believer to speak in an unknown tongue, whether it is the heavenly language, or a foreign language not known to the speaker. The gift is diverse in operation, which means the tongues operate in various or different ways. The Bible refers to new tongues, other tongues, diverse kinds of tongues and unknown tongues. The gift has several purposes, depending on the operation. There is the gift of tongues in public meetings given for a sign to those unbelieving. The gift of tongues used in a public meeting along with an interpretation is also considered prophecy. When Peter preached at Cornelius's house, the evidence of tongues was a sign of being baptized in the Holy Spirit. Tongues are also for prayer and praise. But please note, speaking in tongues is not the Holy Spirit. It is the evidence and manifestation of the indwelling of the Holy Spirit. The supernatural gift of tongues is the language of spiritual worship, intercession and personal edification. Paul refers to the gift of tongues as the language of heaven. Divers kinds of tongues is the most scrutinized spiritual gift. For this reason, I feel it's important to spend extra time educating on the subject while reviewing supporting scripture.

The gift of Diverse Kinds of Tongues in Scripture:

(Isaiah 28:11 NKJV) *"For with stammering lips and another tongue He will speak to this people,"*

(Mark 16:17 NKJV) *"And these signs will follow those who believe: In My name they will cast out demons; they will speak with new tongues."*

(Romans 8:26 NLT) *"And the Holy Spirit helps us in our weakness. For example, we don't know what God wants us to pray for. But the Holy Spirit prays for us with groaning's that cannot be expressed in words."*

(1 Corinthians 12:28 NLT) *"Here are some of the parts God has appointed for the church; - - those who speak in unknown languages."*

(1 Corinthians 14:2, 4-5, 14-15, 22 NKJV) *"2 For he who speaks in a tongue does not speak to men but to God, for no one understands him; however, in the spirit he speaks mysteries. 4 He who speaks in a tongue edifies himself, but he who prophesies edifies the church. 5 I wish you all spoke with tongues. 14 For if I pray in a tongue, my spirit prays, but my understanding is unfruitful. 15 What is the conclusion then? I will pray with the spirit, and I will also pray with understanding. I will sing with the spirit, and I will also sing with the understanding. 22 Therefore, tongues are for a sign, not to those who believe but to unbelievers;"*

(Jude 20 NLT) *"But you, beloved, must build each other up in your most holy faith, pray in the power of the Holy Spirit,"*

(Ephesians 6:18 NKJV) *"Praying always with all prayer and supplication in the Spirit."*

(1 Corinthians 13:1 NKJV) *"Though I speak with the tongues of men and of angels, but have not love,"*

The gift of Diverse Kinds of Tongues in action:

(Acts 2:4 NKJV) *"And they were all filled with the Holy Spirit and began to speak with other tongues, as the Spirit gave them utterance.*

(Acts 10:44-46 NKJV) *"While Peter was still speaking these words, the Holy Spirit fell upon all those who heard the word. ⁴⁵ And those of the circumcision who believed were astonished, as many as came with Peter, because the gift of the Holy Spirit had been poured out on the Gentiles also. ⁴⁶ For they heard them speak with tongues and magnify God.*

(Acts 19:6 NKJV) *"And when Paul had laid hands on them, the Holy Spirit came upon them, and they spoke with tongues and prophesied.*

What is the purpose of speaking in tongues? In studying the above scripture, we find three specific purposes.

A. Speaking in tongues is the evidence of the baptism of the Holy Spirit / Ghost.

B. The gift of diverse kinds of tongues is for prayer and praise.

C. Tongues accompanied with interpretation is for a sign to the unbeliever.

9. Interpretation of Tongues

The interpretation of tongues is the verbalization of the meaning of a message delivered in an unknown language or diverse kinds of tongues. This message will follow the gift of tongues, giving the intended message to those who are to hear. The interpretation is not an exact translation of the message in tongues. The gift of interpretation is to give the part of the message God wants us to hear and understand. This gift gives you the essence of the message, not a word–for–word translation. That is why you may hear a long message in tongues followed by a short interpretation of that message. Divers kinds of tongues along with the interpretation of tongues is used for a sign to the unbeliever.

10

What Does It Look Like

What does it look like to be radically changed by the power and love of God? What does it look like to live in the fullness of the Holy Spirit? What does it look like when one is consumed by the Godhead? Man lived for thousands of years without being able to fully answer this question. Countless men and women devoted to the God of Abraham, Isaac, and Jacob, without the breath of the Godhead. Today, we have been breathed upon by all three. How can we ever complain when countless souls prevailed with only the knowledge and breath of God the Father? What does it look like to be breathed on by all three members of the Godhead? What happens when you receive life, salvation, and power? One thing is for certain, you will not remain the same, but you will experience radical change. The breath of God is not meant to leave you the same. We are to be changed into the image of the Son of God through His provided atonement and the power of the Holy Spirit. No change means you have not been fully breathed upon. To answer the question, we must go back to where it all started.

> **(Acts 2:40–47 NKJV)** *"And with many other words he testified and exhorted them, saying, "Be saved from this perverse generation." ⁴¹ Then those who gladly received his word were baptized; and that day about three thousand souls were added to them. And they continued steadfastly in the apostles' doctrine and fellowship, in the breaking of bread, and in prayers. Then fear came upon every soul, and many wonders and signs were done through the apostles. Now all who believed were together, and had all things in common, and sold their possessions and goods, and divided them among all, as anyone had need. So continuing daily with one accord in the temple, and breaking bread from house to house, they ate their food with gladness and simplicity of heart, ⁴⁷ praising God and having favor with all the people. And the Lord added to the church daily those who were being saved."*

According to this text, it looks like a revival. With many words, those breathed upon began to proclaim and testify of the gospel and were compelled to share the good news of Jesus Christ with a desire to see transformation. The 120 in the upper room were filled with the fullness of the Godhead. More than words, they emulated the power of the Holy Spirit with evidence. Their Spirit-filled boldness, testimonies and preaching of the gospel added over 3,000 souls in one day. The evidence of being breathed upon by the Godhead looked like 3,000 souls being added to the kingdom. What was the difference? The disciples had most likely spoken to this same group of people many times before. It is unlikely that most of the 3,000 were just hearing of Jesus for the first time. They were probably very familiar with Jesus, His disciples and their ministry. Some of these people could have very well been in the crowd yelling, "crucify him." Why are they now being saved by the thousands and why are they now receiving Jesus after He's now gone? The difference is power. The difference is God given authority. The difference is they were no longer speaking from within themselves. The difference is now they've been breathed upon by the Godhead. The same preachers preaching the same message, but now they had the Holy Spirit testifying through them. Now their words carried anointing. Now the message carried power. Now the Holy Spirit was drawing the hearers into the loving presence of a risen savior. The 120 no longer performed ministry as a duty. Now the Holy Spirit used them as human instruments to accomplish the will of the Father. My friend, 3,000 souls in one day is the difference in being baptized in the Holy Spirit with evidence verses ministry without the Spirit. Ministry without the Spirit bears no fruit. Ministry in the Spirit bears uncalculatable fruit. It looks like the manifested evidence of the power of the Holy Spirit.

In the above text of Acts 2, verse 42 gives us what's known as the Apostles Doctrine, four fundamental devotions establishing the church. The first is doctrine or teaching. The foundation of the ministry was to gain knowledge and wisdom of the Word. As before mentioned, the Word is God breathed. It is our sword. The charge is to study to show yourself approved. You can't teach and preach the gospel without knowing the Word. Studying was a normal part of their daily routine. Secondly, they wanted to be people of God in continuous fellowship. Often overlooked today an inconvenience. A fellowship is a society in partnership, a community or brotherhood. The word fellowship here means a unity brought about by the Holy Spirit. Once again, we see the need and desire for unity among the brethren. The early church devoted themselves to communication and unity with God and with each other. This unified fellowship is more than just casual gatherings. This is a spiritual communion orchestrated by the Holy Spirit. We are to be in fellowship with each other and the Godhead simultaneously. Thirdly, this unity brings the breaking of bread. Christians have been eating together since the beginning of the church. This breaking of bread was believed to be sharing a meal and partaking in Eucharist, or the Lord's Supper. There is a consistent recognizing of God in all things. The last of the four devotions was prayer. Prayer for their ministry, prayer for those who would be hearing and prayer for the continual refilling of the Holy Spirit. The baptism of the Holy Spirit changed everything. They once followed Jesus but now that He's ascended they followed the leading of the Spirit, praying in Jesus name. With the Spirit's guidance, they learn what's most important for their ministry. Study to show yourself approved.

> **(2 Timothy 2:15b NKJV)** *"rightly dividing the word of truth."*

Be unified as one body, fellowship. Meet your physical need of food while recognizing the one who meets all our needs, breaking of bread. Never go alone, always seek the will, power, and direction of the Spirit, prayer.

The ministry of the early church continued with many signs and wonders with a continued display of the manifested power. They grew stronger in unity while continuing in the Apostles Doctrine. This Spirit-led outline for ministry brought great success, adding to the church daily. Great revival may start with 2 Chronicles 7:14, but it doesn't stop there. We must allow the Holy Spirit to lead us in doctrine, fellowship, breaking of bread and prayer.

By What Power or By What Name

The New Covenant church of Acts is what we should emulate today. God has not changed, people have. Luke wrote the book of Acts, inspired by the breath of God, to give those who follow a road map. The testimony of the church should be signs, wonders, salvation, love, transformation and forgiveness. Anything less is a disappointment and a failure.

We see the continued manifestation in chapters 3 and 4 of Acts. Chapter 3 begins with the first written and recorded notable miracle performed after the ascension of Jesus. Peter and John are entering the temple when they come across a young man who was lame on his feet. Laying by the gate, called Beautiful, was common for this man as he laid daily. I ponder just how long and how often this man laid by the gate. The text refers to him as man, not a boy or child. Since he is an adult he must be at least 20 years of age. So, possibly upwards of twenty years or more this man laid by the gate asking for alms.

> **(Acts 3:6-10 NKJV)** *"Then Peter said, "Silver and gold I do not have, but what I do have I give you: In the name of Jesus Christ of Nazareth, rise up and walk." And he took him by the right hand and lifted him up, and immediately his feet and ankle bones received strength. So he, leaping up, stood and walked and entered the temple with them— walking, leaping, and praising God. And all the people saw him walking and praising God. Then they knew that it was he who sat begging alms at the Beautiful Gate of the temple; and they were filled with wonder and amazement at what had happened to him."*

Peter and John now walked in a new power and anointing since being baptized in the Holy Spirit.

Scripture makes it clear that the religious leaders were not intrigued to hear that disciples were now able to do the same type miracles that Jesus did. They thought killing Jesus would put an end to the supernatural wonders. To their surprise, miracles continued, and the preaching of Jesus Christ increased. Their response was to arrest Peter and John to put an end to this preaching. Although the supernatural was evident in the new church the religious leaders attempted to suppress the movement with continued arrest and threats.

> **(Acts 4:7-10 NKJV)** *"And when they had set them in the midst, they asked, "By what power or by what name have you done this?" Then Peter, filled with the Holy Spirit, said to them, "Rulers of the people and elders of Israel: If we this day are judged for a good deed done to a helpless man, by what means he has been made well, let it be known to you all, and to all the people of Israel, that by the name of Jesus Christ of Nazareth, whom you crucified, whom God raised from the dead, by Him this man stands here before you whole."*

Can you image the boldness in Peter? He stood in the power of the Holy Spirit and assigned the miracle of signs and wonders to Jesus. He proclaimed that their attempt to crucify Jesus actually released a far greater power by His resurrection. Peter declared the source of their abilities was in the name of Jesus. Peter proclaimed in boldness, "the man you crucified, whom God raised from the dead." Wow! The content of this scene is amazing. The baptism of the Holy Spirit had empowered them to do as Jesus did. Not only did they answer their question in boldness, they preached the gospel to the very people who killed Jesus.

> **(Acts 4:12 NKJV)** *"Nor is there salvation in any other, for there is no other name under heaven given among men by which we must be saved."*

True Holy Spirit baptism will bring to light the ignorance and intent of the enemy.

> **(Acts 4:13 NJV)** *"13 Now when they saw the boldness of Peter and John, and perceived that they were uneducated and untrained men, they marveled. And they realized that they had been with Jesus."*

I love the response, "they realized they had been with Jesus." The religious leaders quickly realized they were possibly dealing with a power that could not be contained. They did later make the attempt in verse 17 to tell them not to speak in that name. Even the unbelieving religious leaders knew there's just something about that name.

> **(Philippians 2:10–11 NKJV)** *"10 that at the name of Jesus every knee should bow, of those in heaven, and of those on earth, and of those under the earth, 11 and that every tongue should confess that Jesus Christ is Lord, to the glory of God the Father."*

11

I Will Pour Out My Spirit

(Acts 2:15-19 NLT) *"These people are not drunk, as some of you are assuming. Nine o'clock in the morning is much too early for that. No, what you see was predicted long ago by the prophet Joel: 'In the last days,' God says, 'I will pour out my Spirit upon all people. Your sons and daughters will prophesy. Your young men will see visions, and your old men will dream dreams. In those days I will pour out my Spirit even on my servants—men and women alike—and they will prophesy. And I will cause wonders in the heavens above and signs on the earth below— blood and fire and clouds of smoke."*

Peter stands to teach and explain this phenomenon to the confused crowd. The behavior exhibited by the committed 120 must have made everyone think they were drunk. Supernatural baptism will cause you to function and act in ways that seem odd to you and those who witness it.

(1 Corinthians 1:27 NKJV) *"²⁷ Instead, God chose things the world considers foolish in order to shame those who think they are wise. And he chose things that are powerless to shame those who are powerful."*

Peter reminds the people that Joel had prophesied an outpouring that would fall on all flesh. This movement comes as predicted and not a surprise. "This is that spoken by the prophet Joel." In other words, the promise has now come. "In the last days," refers to the era of the church from Pentecost until the return of Christ. Under the New Covenant the outpouring of the Spirit is for all flesh. The definition of pour is to flow or move continuously in a steady stream. A supernatural dispensation for all who believe. The promise is to men and women, young and old. No one is excluded. Unfortunately, many teach that particular genders and even races cannot operate in this powerful outpouring. Let's not be ignorant here. The Scripture does not make a mistake in saying "I will pour out my Spirit upon all flesh." If you are a believer, if you are surrendered and obedient, all Christians both male and female fall within the description of all flesh. The prophecy of the steady outpouring flow gives insight to some of the gifts that will be in continuous operation. They will prophesy, have dreams and vision, and there will be signs and wonders.

There are two groups of believers, those who want the outpouring of the Spirit and those who want to attend church without the disruption of a spiritual movement. The Lord desires to pour out His Spirit and breathe on all who will seek Him. The Spirit desires to flow. Congregations cannot settle for a drip when they experience the moisture of the Spirit. Don't settle for a seasonal rain when the Lord wants to pour continuously in a steady stream. Will you consecrate yourself for a continual outpouring or will you settle for the seasonal rain?

All historic revivals and awakenings have common threads of the moving and operating of the Holy Spirit. The Frontier revivals with John Edwards in the 1790's; the charismatic movements with Kathryn Kulman and Kenneth Hagin in the 1970's, the Brownsville and Toronto revivals in the 1990's. There are reported current outpourings such as thousands being saved daily in China and Muslims dreaming of Jesus. What did the movements have in common? The common thread is that all these movements contained unified obedient groups of desperately hungry people who prayed in confession and Spirit while seeking the very heart of God. All great movements met the prerequisites we've previously mentioned. Are we willing to submit once again to the Apostles Doctrine and the guiding outline of 2 Chronicles 7:14? The Azusa Street revival, 1906 – 1915, restored Pentecostal outpourings in America. The Los Angeles Daily Times had an article from April 18, 1906 about William J. Seymour and the Azusa Street Revival. *"According to the Los Angeles Times, a bizarre new religious sect had started with people "breathing strange utterances and mouthing a creed which it would seem no sane mortal could understand." Furthermore, "Devotees of the weird doctrine practice the most fanatical rites, preach the wildest theories, and work themselves into a state of mad excitement." If that didn't grab the reader's attention, the article continued by saying that, "Colored people and a sprinkling of whites compose the congregation, and night is made hideous in the neighborhood by the howling's of the worshippers who spend hours swaying forth and back in a nerve-racking attitude of prayer and supplication. To top it all off, they claimed to have received the "gift of tongues," and what's more, "comprehend the babel." Nonetheless, for the spiritually hungry who came from far and wide to receive their Pentecost, "the very atmosphere of heaven" had descended, according to one. A visiting Baptist pastor said, "The Holy Spirit fell upon me and filled me literally, as it seemed to lift me up, for indeed, I was in the air in an instant, shouting, 'Praise God,' and instantly I began to speak in another language."*

This article gives us a view of what others see when they witness the outpouring of the Holy Spirit. This worldly view is why Peter had to explain that they were not drunk. O how I pray we can once again look like the Holy Spirit baptism of Acts and the Revival of Azusa Street. Can we once again forget about gender, race and age? Inviting the Holy Spirit to baptize us with a fresh outpouring.

Even Greater Works

(John 14:12-16 NASB) *"Truly, truly, I say to you, he who believes in Me, the works that I do, he will do also; and greater works than these he will do; because I go to the Father. Whatever you ask in My name, that will I do, so that the Father may be glorified in the Son. If you ask Me anything in My name, I will do it. "If you love Me, you will keep My commandments. I will ask the Father, and He will give you another Helper, that He may be with you forever;"*

The promise is not that the followers of Jesus would perform greater works in value, but in scope and number. Jesus' ministry was limited to just over three years, but the same Spirit and gifts continue to be multiplied through Holy Spirit baptism, empowering believers. Jesus wants us to be great for the kingdom, but not for vain glory. Every manifested work accomplished in the name of Jesus is to edify the body and compel unbelievers to receive Christ. We should not take this as a right for competition but as a right to truly be Christ-like. He tells us twice in this text that anything we ask in His name will be done. We make the petition, accrediting the promise to His name, and He does the work. Many have difficulty receiving the validity of this text, but faith will cause you to accept the Word of God as truth.

> **(Mark 9:23 NKJV)** *"Jesus said to him, If you can believe, all things are possible to him who believes."*

> **(Matthew 19:26 NKJV)** *"But Jesus looked at them and said to them, with men this is impossible, but with God all things are possible."*

When faith arises, greater works persist. We are endued with the same Spirit and anointing that Jesus had. When we accept this call and walk in this anointing we will see greater works increasing, so that the Father may be glorified in the Son. Ask Him today to prepare you for greater works. Ask Him to increase your faith. Pray and ask to be baptized in the Holy Spirit. If you can believe, greater works will become common in your walk with God. Make no mistake about it, Jesus desires for you to be baptized in the Spirit with evidence. He wants your sphere to be greater than His.

Waiting with Anticipation

God wants you to have the gifts He's promised in scripture. The key to obtaining many of these promises is the ability to wait. I know it's true, no one likes to wait. The real challenge in waiting is our misunderstanding of what it actually means. Our natural instinct is to believe that waiting is simply not getting what we want and need when we want and need it. The given image of waiting is that of a person sitting in a dark room staring at dark walls while they go without what they seek. This misunderstanding has caused many to abort the promises of God rather than waiting for them.

> **(James 1:4 NKJV)** *"But let patience have its perfect work, that you may be perfect and complete, lacking nothing."*

Waiting on God is granting Him permission to work on you in the process. The result of waiting is for Him to perfect you and complete the work He started. When His work is over you will lack nothing. Waiting is easy when our focus is on the end result and not the current absence of what we seek. The actual biblical definition of wait is to have faith and hope while remaining in readiness and expectation. Like waiting, patience is more than just sitting around waiting for something. Patience is biblically defined as having the ability to wait without complaint, waiting with expectation. Receiving this perspective should change our attitude when being patient with God while He's doing His work. It's important not to forget that patience is a characteristic of love and a virtue of the fruit of the Spirit. People sign up for college knowing it will take work, time and money. They are willing to do this because they focus on the end result and not the daily routine. Finishing college comes with a final expectation that propels you forward in life. Parents pray about the perfect time to conceive a child. But we all know that conception is just the beginning of the process. You will need to carry that gift for nine months before it actually becomes yours to hold. We are willing to wait even though we know the process could possibly be very uncomfortable for the one carrying the promise. Again, our focus is not on the daily wait but the end result. Waiting is all about keeping faith and hope on the end result and knowing that God is completing a work as you wait. If you are unwilling to wait, you forfeit the right to graduate with a degree. If you are unwilling to wait, you abort the promise or possibly cause a miscarriage resulting in the loss of the spectacular end result. I'm not trying to mislead you to think that waiting is easy. Waiting is never easy. However, waiting becomes manageable when we know He's creating something far greater than we can imagine. It becomes easier when we focus on the result rather than what we have yet to obtain. His promise is that at the end of waiting you will lack nothing and be complete. Now, I don't know about you, but I think that's a promise worth waiting for. Just repeat this thought, "He wants me to lack nothing." But don't forget, this will require you to wait and allow Him to complete His work.

> **(Lamentations 3:25 NKJV)** *"The Lord is good to those who wait for Him, to the soul that seeks Him."*

> **(Isaiah 40:31 NKJV)** *"But those who wait on the Lord shall renew their strength; they shall mount up with wings like eagles, they shall run and not be weary, they shall walk and not faint."*

Correctly defining wait should allow you to see this verse in a new and promising way. Those who continue in hope and faith will renew their strength. Those who allow God to work on them while they enter a new season will develop supernatural rest and power. I want to use this verse to debunk the idea of being miserable and depressed while waiting. You'll notice that the text goes on to say that those waiting are running and walking. In other words, though they are waiting, they keep on keeping on. Life doesn't stop while we wait. Neither does ministry and our service for the Lord. Rather, this text gives encouragement that you won't run on empty while waiting. God's continued work on you will not allow you to become weary in doing good, nor will He allow you to faint in exhaustion. The encouragement is to have an expected outcome.

> **(Galatians 6:9 NKJV)** *"And let us not grow weary while doing good, for in due season we shall reap if we don't lose heart."*

We are to remain in expectant anticipation when we can't see the end result. We are to remain in steadfast faith even when we can't see the promise. We are commanded to wait in hope even if hope seems lost. Remembering that His final promise is that we will lack nothing and be complete. Waiting yet running, waiting yet walking, waiting but still praying, giving, going, loving and serving. The fulfilled promises are only for those who will wait on the Lord. If you have been waiting in hope and faith, get ready and expect your due season.

> **(Psalm 40:1-3 NLT)** *"1. I waited patiently for the Lord to help me, and He turned to me and heard my cry. 2. He lifted me out of the pit of despair, out of the mud and the mire. He set my feet on solid ground and steadied me as I walked along. 3. He has given me a new song to sing, a hymn of praise to our God."*

The Union of Believers

God seeks a body of believers who are willing to be many, yet united as one. A body willing and desiring to be sanctified and consecrated, holy and set apart for the purpose of the Father. Holy Spirit is restricted until the body of Christ is free from division, free from favoritism, from of envy, free from strife, free of personal agendas, and free of jealousy. God seeks an ecclesia whole in unity and consecrated for the work of the Lord. The union of believes is the prerequisite for an outpouring of God's glory.

In chapter 3, there was a brief paragraph about whole unity. I think it's important to pick up that conversation again to detail the significance of the need for unity. Scripture makes it clear that without unity very little can be accomplished. Corporate manifestations of glory and revival only happen in the union of believers in unity. If we fail at corporate unity, we will fail in our attempt of obtaining all God has for us.

We have spent much time learning about the gifts of the Godhead. Scripture shows us that unity is required for each to function properly and at full capacity. The gifts of the Father, the gifts of the Son, and the gifts of the Holy Spirit all give scriptural necessity for a unified state of harmony and oneness. Immediately before listing the gifts of the Father we read a command for unity.

> **(Romans 12:4-5 KNJV)** *4. For as we have many members in one body, but all the members do not have the same function, 5. So we, being many, are one body in Christ, and individually members of one another.*

We read the same command immediately following the giving of the gifts of the Son.

> **(Ephesians 4:13 NLT)** *This will continue until we all come to such unity in our faith and knowledge of God's Son that we will be mature in the Lord, measuring up to the full and complete standard of Christ.*

And not surprisingly, we see the same requirement and need for unity immediately following the gifts of the Spirit.

> **(1 Cor 12:12 NKJV)** *For as the body is one and has many members, but all the members of that one body, being many, are one body, so also is Christ.*

Make no mistake; failure in unity will result in failure of accomplishment. Proper functionality of all gifts and all corporate manifestations require unity.

12

The Will of Holy Spirit

The Holy Spirit is the third person of the trinity. He is not a thing, He is not an it. He is the presence of God on earth. Many are too quick to overlook the significance of this person. Some overly zealous charismatics have forgotten the God and glorified the gifts. Other congregations have no knowledge of whether the Holy Spirit is active in their lives or not. This opinion is not a myth. I participated at one time in glorifying the gifts until I learned truth. The gifts are magnificent. However, there would be no gifts without the distributor of the gifts. The Spirit is a person and the gifts are His manifestations. I perceive in these last days we have grown in wisdom and changed our thinking. I see a return in the pursuance of the Holy Spirit like never before.

> **(1 Corinthians 12:11 NKJV)** *"But one and the same Spirit works all these things, distributing to each one individually as He wills."*

The Holy Spirit has been given full authority to give and distribute the nine spiritual gifts as He wills.

(1 Corinthians 12:7 NKJV) *"But the manifestation of the Spirit is given to each one for the profit of all."*

The Holy Spirit lives in you. He knows you better than you know yourself. He moved in and took up residency the moment you received Jesus as your Savior. He is your compass. He knows your strengths and weaknesses. He is familiar with your character; your fruit. There is nothing in your resume that He is not aware of. He knows the end from the beginning. He knows the good and the bad. He knows what you've repented of and what you may still be unrepentant of today. His knowledge of you is why God has given the Holy Spirit sole discretion when it comes to distributing gifts. Only the Spirit knows what you are capable of spiritually. It is His responsibility to place each member in the body as He sees fit. Gifts are given by the Spirit and they are nurtured by the office gifts of the fivefold ministry.

Many churches and ministries promote their ability to teach one how to obtain a gift. There is a fine line between teaching someone how to use a gift and teaching how to imitate a gift. Imitation is dangerous and contrary to the will of God. The Holy Spirit grants gifts when you repent and are baptized. Once you've done this you seek the Holy Spirit to give you the gifts as He wills, not as you will. Be mindful that the Spirit desires and is pleased to distribute gifts. It's not something He does begrudgingly. He wants to give you gifts. Don't allow the enemy or yourself to complicate the process. You are worthy to receive the gifts the Holy Spirit wants you to have. If you weren't ready or worthy, He wouldn't give them to you. If you haven't received spiritual gifts yet, begin now to prepare yourself. He's ready to give when you're ready to receive.

How Important Is He

(Mark 3:28-29 NKJV) *"28 Assuredly, I say to you, all sins will be forgiven the sons of men, and whatever blasphemies they may utter; 29 but he who blasphemes against the Holy Spirit never has forgiveness, but is subject to eternal condemnation."*

Blasphemy against the Holy Spirit is to deny and speak against the Holy Spirit; denying Him and refusing to accept Him. Blasphemy against the Holy Spirit is the sin which is unforgivable, the unpardonable sin. The Holy Spirit is so important that denying Him is the only unpardonable sin. Jesus wanted to make a statement here and He wanted everyone to understand without confusion. All sins ever committed can and will be forgiven. Murder, adultery, lying and cheating are all forgivable. Only one sin is beyond the grace of God, to deny and come against the third person of the trinity, the Holy Spirit. To deny the Holy Spirit is to deny the deity of the Father and the Son. The religious leaders were crediting the miracles of Jesus to the work of satan. (Read Mark 3 and Matthew 12) Let's look at the Mark account from the Amplified version for better clarity.

(Mark 3:29-30 AMP) *"29 but whoever blasphemes against the Holy Spirit and His power [by attributing the miracles done by Me to satan] never has forgiveness, but is guilty of an everlasting sin [a sin which is unforgivable in this present age as well as in the age to come]" 30 [Jesus*

> *said this] because the scribes and Pharisees were [attributing
> His miracles to satan by] saying, He has an unclean spirit."*

There is an eternal charge in denying the Holy Spirit. I lament over the international trend of church services without Spirit. Just as the Pharisees convinced the crowd to deny Jesus, churches are again convincing crowds to deny the Holy Spirit. Blasphemy is now concealed in the mirage of seeker friendly comfort. They invite you to come. They invite you to have some coffee. Maybe they invite you to have a bagel but be assured they will not inconvenience you with the manifestation of the Holy Spirit. Please understand, I'm certainly not suggesting that churches who serve coffee don't have the Spirit. My focus is the danger of some making food and drink more enticing than the Spirit. My attempt is for us to realize we should be chasing God rather than the beverages offered at church. I only mention this because I've had people ask, which church offers coffee? My friend, I beg you to never lose your desire for the Holy Spirit.

> **(1 John 5:16b–17 NLT)** *"But there is a sin that leads
> to death, and I am not saying you should pray for those who
> commit it. 17 All wicked actions are sin, but not every sin
> leads to death."*

One cannot receive salvation unless the Spirit draws him. If you deny the Spirit, you forfeit salvation and eternal life in heaven.

> **(John 6:44 NKJV)** *"No one can come to Me unless the
> Father who sent Me draws him; and I will raise him up at
> the last day."*

Keep the Fire Burning

To experience the fullness of the Spirit we must live submitted to the Spirit. You cannot live submitted to the Spirit and gratify the flesh at the same time. The Spirit and the flesh oppose one another. Submitting to the Spirit requires circumcision of the flesh. You must cut away the need to gratify fleshly desires. The Bible provides a plethora of scripture teaching us how to deny the flesh.

> **(Galatians 2:20 NKJV)** *"I have been crucified with Christ; it is no longer I who live, but Christ lives in me; and the life which I now live in the flesh I live by faith in the Son of God, who loved me and gave Himself for me."*

Why would you ever want to hinder the Holy Spirit, the most powerful force on the planet? We need to keep the fire of the Holy Spirit burning.

> **(Romans 12:1 NLT)** *"I plead with you to give your bodies to God because of all He has done for you. Let them be a living and holy sacrifice — the kind He will find acceptable. This is truly the way to worship Him."*

I am the temple of the Holy Spirit and He is within me at all times. My actions can limit, hinder and insult the Spirit's ability to work in me, and through me. When I gratify the flesh, the Holy Spirit must work on me rather than being able to work through me. How often does He want to minister through me to others but He's busy ministering to me because I haven't circumcised the flesh? The Holy Spirit is always at work, either on me or through me. Always be mindful that what you see He sees and what you hear

He hears. My intake and output impact the Holy Spirit's ability to move through me.

> **(1 Thessalonians 5:19 AMP)** *"Do not quench [subdue, or be unresponsive to the working and guidance of] the Holy Spirit."*

The only reason Scripture tells us not to hinder the Spirit is because we can. You can hinder the Spirit. You can subdue, suppress or limit Him. The Holy Spirit is very sensitive. Actions, behavior and disobedience limits and hinders the Spirit's ability to minister through the human vessel. He will never force Himself on human beings. You control and decide the Spirit's access in your life. Imagine the victorious achievements the Holy Spirit could accomplish if He were never limited.

> **(Ephesians 4:30 NKJV)** *"And do not grieve the Holy Spirit of God, by whom you were sealed for the day of redemption."*

To grieve means to trouble, disappoint or insult. All these emotions make this feel like a romance novel. We are created so precisely in the likeness of the Godhead that we humans seem to share similar emotions to that of the Holy Spirit. Few ever take time to consider the feelings of the Holy Spirit. Why does God love to be worshipped? He loves how it feels. God took pleasure in creation. Jesus wept over Jerusalem and Lazarus. The Holy Spirit can be quenched and grieved. It feels strange to write this but don't hurt His feelings.

We disappoint the Spirit when we do things we know we shouldn't do. We insult the Spirit when He tells us not to do something and we refuse to listen to His advice. Such actions contradict our desire for Him to dwell within us. Reading the Scripture from Ephesians 4:20-32, you see the contrast of the old man verses the new man. We are to conquer the old sinful corrupt ways while being renewed, putting on the new man and changing from glory to glory. Replace lying with truth. Replace anger with brief righteousness indignation. Stop stealing and replace it with honest work. Replace foul language with gracious speech. Such behavior will grieve and quench the Holy Spirit. We are to replace those old sinful behaviors with kindness, tenderheartedness and forgiveness. You can receive an increase of the Holy Spirit as you grow in God and as you seek for more. You can lose the Holy Spirit by your actions and behaviors. He will not dwell in unholy temples and He will not fellowship with unholy behavior.

I want to pause here for some encouragement. Many churches are blessed to have multiple gifts in operation. It should be the goal of every church to have all nine spiritual gifts in full operation. It should be our goal to have multiple people with multiple gifts. To say, we have five gifts in our church is the same as saying we are operating at half of God's promised fullness. You may be reading this and realizing you have been gifted by the Holy Spirit but you're not fulfilling the call. The church and the Kingdom needs you to stir up the gift of God within you. Gifts unused are dead gifts. God anointed you for the benefit of His people, use what He gave you.

(2 Timothy 1:6 NKJV) *"Therefore I remind you to stir up the gift of God which is in you through the laying on of my hands."*

Spiritual Life Support

Spiritual forces exist in your life. Right now, you are giving life support to spiritual forces. Spirits must have life support. Holy and righteous Spirits as well as evil spirits exist. Are you entertaining the Spirit or spirits? The life you live, your atmosphere, your environment, your words, all give life to the Spirit or spirits. There are evil spirits just like there is the Holy Spirit. **(1 Timothy 1:7 NKJV)** *"For God has not given us a spirit of fear, but of power and of love and of a sound mind."* Fear is an evil spirit. Through His Spirit He has given us power, love and a sound mind.

> **(Romans 8:2, 14-15 NKJV)** *"2 For the law of the Spirit of the life in Christ Jesus has made me free from the law of sin and death. 14 For as many as are led by the Spirit of God, these are the sons of God. 15 For you did not receive the spirit of bondage again to fear, but you received the Spirit of adoption by whom we cry out, Abba, Father."*

Evil spirits are not God given. They are spread by the enemy and allowed to inhabit people through actions, behaviors, disobedience and unbelief. Entertaining evil spirits give them permission to stay. Entertaining the Holy Spirit drives away evil spirits. You are giving life support to either spirits or the Spirit. Live in the light, a life pleasing to God, and you will give life to the Spirit and drive out spirits. Do not grieve or quench the Holy Spirit. He is your only ally in keeping spirits at bay. Therefore, it is important to have the spiritual gift of discerning of spirits.

(Romans 8:6 NKJV) *"For to be carnally minded is death, but to be spiritually minded is life and peace."*

Evil spirits are sent by their commander to steal, kill and destroy. The Holy Spirit has come to build and empower the believer to a life of victory in Jesus Christ.

13

He's Not Finished with Me

Have you ever failed God? Have you ever failed in your attempt to please Him? Have you ever contemplated relinquishing your relationship with Him because you felt inadequate? Have you ever deemed yourself unworthy to be called His child? Do you feel unqualified to fulfill the assignment He's given you? Most all Christians have experienced a season of doubt when we would say yes to these questions. We have failed in pleasing Him and we've failed in not committing sin. Inadequacy is often experienced each time God gives us a new assignment or we are able to reach a new level in Him. Our failures demand we feel unworthy, our inadequacies demand we feel unqualified. Now that we've given our opinions, what does He say. I don't think God counts our failed attempts. I know He doesn't keep track of repented sin. I believe His interest is whether or not we keep going and keep trying. In Him, failures are forgotten. In Him, Sin is forgiven. In Him, the unqualified are qualified. In Him, the unworthy are made worthy. God didn't breathe on us so that we could quit the race every time something goes wrong. He breathed on us so that we could serve Him continually and faithfully with power in Spirit. No matter what your thoughts are, He's not finished with you yet. Until you leave this world in death, the race is not over, and you have not finished pouring out. A container is not empty until it's poured out.

> **(2 Timothy 4:6 NKJV)** *"For I am already being poured out as a drink offering, and the time of my departure is at hand."*

Paul did not make this declaration until his assignments were complete and his race was over. Until your assignments are complete, He's not finished with you. We must move beyond our failures and our way of thinking. God has a work to complete and He's waiting for His willing vessels to arise to the occasion. This is the day to declare that you haven't yet poured out and He's not finished.

The Bible reveals story after story of the failures of its historic figures. Jacob frequently lied and deceived to get his way. David committed many sins while striving to serve God. Moses committed murder, Jonah ran from God, and the Israelites spent forty years disobeying basic instructions. Failure did not depict the end of the story. God has a way of taking the brokenness of man to create the beauty of His unfailing love.

> **(Matthew 4:18–20 NKJV)** *18. And Jesus, walking by the Sea of Galilee, saw two brothers, Simon called Peter, and Andrew his brother, casting their nets into the sea; for they were fishermen. 19. Then He said to them, "Follow Me, and I will make you fishers of men." 20. They immediately left their nets and followed Him."*

Peter experienced a sudden call to be a disciple of Jesus. In reality, he wasn't sure what this task entailed. Regardless, he immediately left his nets to follow in pursuit. When Jesus calls, we go. The study of Peter shows many ups and downs, victories and defeats. His strength was that he had unwavering boldness. Experience teaches that our greatest strengths can also be our greatest weakness. Peters strong boldness often resulted in manly stubbornness. This stubbornness would bring him to a result that he'd never forget.

> **(Matthew 26:33–35 NKJV)** *"33. Peter answered and said to Him, "Even if all are made to stumble because of You, I will never be made to stumble." 34. Jesus said to him, "Assuredly I say to you that this night, before the rooster crows, you will deny Me three times." 35. Peter said to Him, "Even if I have to die with you, I will not deny You!"*

I'm sure Peter thought, "You can't be serious. I will deny Jesus, a rooster will crow, give me a break." Forward just a couple hours, Jesus has been arrested and brought before the counsel for trial. It's late and everyone is filled with confusion and intense anger. The priest is yelling, the elders are mad, and they need testimony against Jesus. Without proper witnesses, the Jewish religious leaders seek false testimony. Everyone knows they are now telling people what they want them to say falsely against Jesus. The anger has reached a climax, the priest furiously rips their clothing. Declaring blasphemy, they hit and spit in Jesus' face, they begin beating and slapping Him. It's clear that His face is beginning to swell and bruise. This crowds anger has risen to a new level, they don't really know why but they follow the leading of the priest and elders. Wait, who is that over there? Peter is now spotted on the courtyard. He now faces three accusations of following Jesus. Each accusation is met with a fierce response, "I do not know Him."

> (**Matthew 26:74 NKJV**) *"Then he began to curse and swear, saying, "I do not know the Man." Immediately a rooster crowed."*

Suddenly, Peter's greatest fear becomes reality. Instant fear grips Peter as he refuses this charge. He relocated himself in the crowd, but he is recognized once again. Without hesitation, he again declares an innocence of the knowledge of Jesus. Fear and pressure demand he decline the accusation. Then it happened again, "You are one of them, you followed Jesus." Fearful intimidation overwhelms him as dreadful anger swells. Instant distress comes with the imposed accusation. The pressure quickly causes him to react, he begins to yell curse words to assure the furious throng he has nothing to do with Jesus. "I do not know the Man!" This brave, strong man who promised just a few hours ago, "I'll never deny you," is now willing to do whatever it takes to distance himself from the Jews king. Immediately the rooster crowed, and anguish becomes his companion. Remorseful failure now fills his broken soul. He remembers the warning Jesus gave him.

> (**Luke 22:31-32 NKJV**) *"And the Lord said, "Simon, Simon! Indeed, Satan has asked for you, that he may sift you as wheat. But I have prayed for you, that your faith should not fail; and when you have returned to Me, strengthen your brethren."*

Peter is consumed with guilt and shame as Jesus is tortured and crucified. He watches from a distance as Jesus is scourged. Tears and regret bring him to the dark side of the street as Jesus passed by attempting to carry His own cross. Screams of agony fill the air as nails secure the sacrifice to the beams. Standing alone behind a tree in the distance, he hears the crucified Savior, "It is finished." The overwhelming speed of thought. He's dead and I've failed. What have I done? Peter, along with the other disciples now seem lost. Each morning brings the constant reminder of his failure. Every time a rooster crows he relives the painful abandonment of denying Jesus.

Contemplating what to do next, the disciples meet privately to discuss their future. Attention is drawn to the noise of someone running toward the hideout. Mary storms in and declares, "He is gone, He is not in the tomb, He is risen." The disciples now filled with excitement and joy, "He is alive." "But wait," Peter thought, "I failed Him, I denied Him, I sinned against Him, what will He think of me?"

Without clear direction Peter returned to what was familiar, he went fishing. In John 21, it was on the shore that Jesus would call Peter once again. Not only did He reveal Himself at the Sea of Tiberias, He came with a plan to restore Peter's failure. In John 21:15-17, Jesus ask Peter three times if he loved Him. Each time Peter answered with a graceful yes. With each yes, Jesus tells Peter, "Feed my sheep." John 21 is the story of redemption and forgiveness. The restoration of Peter is Jesus saying, "I'm not finished with you." In his weakness, Peter denied Jesus three times. In weakness, he failed three times. But on the shore of the Sea of Tiberias, weakness and failure meet mercy and grace. Three times he failed and three times he was restored. Jesus asked him three times, "do you love Me?" This is agape love; a love Webster cannot properly define. Each time Peter proclaimed his love for Jesus, mercy and grace covered his sin of denial. Mercy and grace covered his weakness. Mercy and grace atoned for his failure. Fully restored, Jesus now gives him the same instruction that He gave him 3 ½ years ago, "Follow Me."

He's Not Finished with Me Yet!

Failure is not your final. Weakness is not your destination. Shame and guilt can be conquered by your risen Savior. Atonement is already provided for repented sin. In other words, He's not finished. You may have denied Him, the rooster may have crowed, but the story is not over. Mercy and grace seek to restore you. He has purpose and assignment waiting to be completed. Forsake what you think, forsake what the world thinks, be restored by what He thinks and by what His Word says.

> **(Romans 8:37-39 NKJV)** *"Yet in all these things we are more than conquerors through Him who loved us. For I am persuaded that neither death not life, nor angels not principalities nor powers, nor things present nor things to come, nor height nor depth, nor any other created thing, shall be able to separate us from the love of God which is in Christ Jesus our Lord."*

> **(1 Peter 5:10 NLT)** *"In His kindness God called you to share in His eternal glory by Christ Jesus, after you have suffered a while, He will restore, support, strengthen you, and He will place you on a firm foundation."*

14

Infiltration of Counterfeit Seed

Satan is nothing more than an imitator. He has been imitating God and His gifts since the beginning of time. He has a counterfeit for everything. Nothing is off limits. Satan's schemes are another reason to be cautious in protecting your anointing. He deceived Eve by twisting a few words from God's command. He even attempted to misquote scripture while temping Jesus but of course that failed. With discerning of spirits, it doesn't take long to identify his use of unspiritual unauthentic people. The old saying says, "everything God has – the devil has a counterfeit."

> **(Matthew 13:24-30 NKJV)** *"24 Another parable He put forth to them, saying: "The kingdom of heaven is like a man who sowed good seed in his field; 25 but while men slept, his enemy came and sowed tares among the wheat and went his way. 26 But when the grain had sprouted and produced a crop, then the tares also appeared. 27 So the servants of the owner came and said to him, 'Sir, did*

> you not sow good seed in your field? How then does it have tares?' 28 He said to them, 'An enemy has done this.' The servants said to him, 'Do you want us then to go and gather them up?' 29 But he said, 'No, lest while you gather up the tares you also uproot the wheat with them. 30 Let both grow together until the harvest, and at the time of harvest I will say to the reapers, "First gather together the tares and bind them in bundles to burn them, but gather the wheat into my barn."

The enemy is always seeking ways to stop God's assignment. He is often successful by imitating and planting look-a-likes to deceive. He has eager intentions, but they can be halted by the Holy Spirit. His plans are easily revealed to those who are anointed and called of God. That's not to say he won't stop in his attempt to deceive God's people.

> **(1 John 4:1 NLT)** *"Dear friends, do not believe everyone who claims to speak by the Spirit. You must test them to see if the spirit they have comes from God. For there are many false prophets in the world."*

Don't allow yourself to become prey to his cheap imitations. This may be redundant, but the only way to test the falseness of your enemy is to have the realness of your God.

(Ephesians 5:1 NKJV) *"Be imitators of God."*

One grave mistake Christians make is expecting their enemy to look like an enemy. Truth is, your enemy will commonly appear in attractive and non-threatening ways. You can read the story of

Samson, Judges 14-16, to learn that his enemy appeared as a sweet beautiful woman. You can only be abandoned by someone close to you. Disloyalty only comes from those who were once loyal. Your adversary, the devil, will generally use people in your inner circle to accomplish his work. Always be mindful of the deceptive trickery of your enemy. Scripture gives a lot of detail on how to test deceptive false imitations. Let's take a look at just a few.

(2 Timothy 3:5 NKJV) *"5 having a form of godliness but denying its power. And from such people turn away."*

Don't be deceived with charisma, fancy words, deceptive tales, large numbers or showmanship. Test every spirit and don't be afraid to turn away. One of the enemy's greatest tools are other people. **(1 Peter 5:8 NKJV)** *"8 Be sober, be vigilant; because your adversary the devil walks about like a roaring lion, seeking whom he may devour."* He presents himself as a roaring lion. This is nothing more than him being an imitator. This is a warning to be watchful because satan may be an imitator, but danger persist in his schemes. Always remember that his objective is to kill, steal, and destroy. Unfortunately, he has been successful in destroying many lives and ministries.

(Matthew 23:2-4 NLT) *"2 The teachers of religious law and the Pharisees are the official interpreters of the law of Moses. 3 So practice and obey whatever they tell you, but don't follow their example. For they don't practice what they teach. 4 They crush people with unbearable religious demands and never lift a finger to ease the burden."*

Jesus takes issue with counterfeit religious leaders demanding the people live and serve God one way while they do the opposite.

Unfortunately, too many good leaders become imitators of the lofted Pharisees. I've known those in the office gifts who were tremendously knowledgeable in hidden mysteries of the Word yet totally ignorant to the basics. They can tell you everything about the book of Revelation but refuse to abide under authority and rebel against all boundaries concerning their gifting. High ranking officers who sit in leadership meetings championing the vision of the church while playing the Absalom card behind closed doors.

> **(3 Timothy 3:7 NKJV)** *"Always learning and never able to come to the knowledge of the truth."*

All counterfeit seed is identified eventually. I remember a leadership meeting in which the Spirit unexpectedly showed up. I was conducting a usual meeting with about twenty-five leaders. The Spirit suddenly spoke through me about leaders not tithing. I was as shocked as they were that the Lord would speak of such a thing in a casual meeting. The Spirit spoke through me, "we cannot preach and lead others to do things we are not doing." There were leaders in that meeting who were championing a vision to be debt free when they themselves were not tithing." I took a deep breath and continued with my agenda. It wasn't long after this meeting that the Lord made me aware of why He said what He did. I do not police tithing in our church. I do not know who does and who does not tithe. Some pastors keep track of tithing members but I chose not to. I believe the Lord confronted our leaders because we were under His direction to become debt free.

> **(Matthew 23:24-27 NLT)** *"Blind guides! You strain your water so you won't accidentally swallow a gnat, but you swallow a camel "What sorrow awaits you teachers of*

religious law and you Pharisees. Hypocrites! For you are so careful to clean the outside of the cup and the dish, but inside you are filthy—full of greed and self-indulgence! You blind Pharisee! First wash the inside of the cup and the dish, and then the outside will become clean, too. "What sorrow awaits you teachers of religious law and you Pharisees. Hypocrites! For you are like whitewashed tombs—beautiful on the outside but filled on the inside with dead people's bones and all sorts of impurity."

Separating the Wolves from the Sheep

A couple years ago I became very weary of disloyalty. I'm content in the statistical fact that most people change the church they attend every three to five years. However, I cannot be content with those who are disloyal and destructive in the process. I've known ministers and leaders who seemingly serve faithfully until their hidden agenda was revealed. Potential doesn't always reveal intention. My sheep were being wounded and I needed to find a way to protect them. I once heard it said, "if you want a snake to reveal itself just place barriers around it." In other words, if you want to find disloyalty and rebellion just require accountability. I would gladly give some great examples here but there's no spoils in doing so.

I took a sabbatical to fast and pray for the purpose of having the Lord speak to me about how to separate the wolves from the sheep, the servants from the rebellious, the willing from the unwilling. I did not expect the response I received from the Lord. I needed to know who was serving for the benefit of the body and who was serving for their own cause. Who is serving because they love the people of God? Who will rebel and defect if their platform is removed? Those serving only for a platform are not serving out of love for the people of God. They are serving out of love for themselves and their ministry. The Lord caused me to think of discipleship. I have always mandated that our leaders need to disciple themselves along with what we supply. I was intense and demanding of the need for personal devotion and discipleship. My desire often landed on deaf ears. The Lord led me to establish a discipleship program. He began to place a vision within me of a program that would require discipleship as a prerequisite for ministry and leadership. I exited that sabbatical with a program called Building Blocks. The program had four levels of completion. The first level was Covenant Membership. Anyone wanting to participate needed to become a member of our church. The reason for membership is commitment. The Lord showed me that if someone wanted to lead or minister to this body they first needed to be committed to the body. Why was I allowing people to lead or minister who were not committed? We do allow participants to read the books in levels two and three for discipleship without becoming members, but they can only graduate if they become a member. The second level was called Covenant Ministry. This level requires the reading of five books with a basic written report for each. It's called Covenant Ministry because in order to be in ministry in our church one must complete this level. These books not only educate and disciple, they cause every person to be in unity as they digest the same material. The third level is called Covenant Influence. This level also required the reading of five books but not the need for written reports. Influence is the essence of leadership. So, in order to be in leadership you needed to complete all three levels, membership, and reading ten books. If you are loyally called and love the people, this requirement is exciting. If you support the leadership and the vision, you're honored to grow in discipleship. I had shared this plan with my staff and elders to get needed feedback. They were all excited about the program and the vision. It wouldn't be easy for some, but they still championed the idea. Five books for ministry and five for leadership seemed like a small request. I planned a meeting with about forty current and potential leaders to share my vision and give the invitation to join. I underestimated the intellectual wisdom of God. Most everyone asked to join with excitement. They gleamed over the potential of growth. However, I had immediate push back from a few in attendance. They were in awe that I would ask them to become members or read books. Can I say this sarcastically, how dare I ask someone to make a commitment to the body or discipleship? This God given program for discipleship accountability has caused a few to leave our church. I never want people to leave our church, but it is necessary sometimes for separation to take place. I was disappointed with the handful of people who chose not to join our vision for discipleship. The program has revealed a few wolves and rebellious spirits that I was overjoyed in their sudden desire to relocate. It is sometimes healthier for a dissolvement and relocation. It's better to separate than experience rebellion or disloyalty. Overall, the program has been a huge success. We've graduated about ninety people in our church. Thus far, most have joined for the desire of discipleship and not leadership or ministry. The program was such a success that the graduates requested further reading. I created a level four called Kingdom Builders. This level was designed for the dedicated participants and required reading twenty-nine books. Level three graduates are not required to join level four but so far, we've graduated about ten participant's and about thirty more working to graduate. I strongly recommend a form of accountability and discipleship for every church.

Evil Seeds

(James 3:13-17 NKJV) *"13 Who is wise and understanding among you? Let him show by good conduct that his works are done in the meekness of wisdom. 14 But if you have bitter envy and self-seeking in your hearts, do not boast and lie against the truth. 15 This wisdom does not descend from above, but is earthly, sensual, demonic. 16 For where envy and self-seeking exist, confusion and every evil thing are there. 17 But the wisdom that is from above is first pure, then peaceable, gentle, willing to yield, full of mercy and good fruits, without partiality and without hypocrisy."*

Whenever God moves, the efforts of the adversary will manifest. The enemy's success exists with humans as willing participants. The enemy seeks to plant seeds that will choke the good seed. Envy, strife, jealousy and anger are evil seeds that give place to confusion, disorder and instability. Just what satan wants, a recipe for disaster. Envy is an evil seed that wants what others have; a painful or resentful awareness of an advantage enjoyed by another and joined with a desire to possess the same advantage. Envy often involves malice along with a desire to cause pain or distress. Strife is an evil seed conjuring conflicts and dissension causing disagreements. Strife leads to discord, disunity, friction, and even warfare. We must rid ourselves of allowing these evil seeds to be successful. We must reveal them rather than partaking.

(Philippians 1:16 NKJV) *"The former preach Christ from selfish ambition, not sincerely, supposing to add affliction to my chains."*

Selfish ambition is within those who care only for themselves. Some regrettably seek promotion and are willing to resort to any method to gain followers.

> **(Philippians 3:18-19 NKJV)** *"18 For many walk, of whom I told you often, and now tell you even weeping, that they are the enemies of the cross of Christ: 19 whose end is destruction, whose god is their belly, and whose glory is in their shame, who set their mind on earthly things."*

Evil seeds are planted for one purpose, to destroy the good. We must identify, reveal and rebuke the evil seeds before they take root.

Evil seeds can destroy a person, ministry or church if not revealed and dealt with. The evil seeds that must be destroyed are envy, strife, selfish ambition, jealousy, anger, resentment, constant criticism, self-promotion, competition and rebellion.

15

~

Pastoring the Prophetic

We now conduct a class in our church called Pastoring the Prophetic. The need for this class came from unforeseen confusion and disruptions. Sometimes church leaders lose focus and think everyone understands how the Holy Spirit operates. Truth is that not everyone does. Not everyone has knowledge of how to even function in their own gift. Without training, the gifts can become chaotic. Not to the fault of the Spirit, but to those attempting to operate in the Spirit without knowledge of order. It's important to know how to use your gift. It's important to know what to do when the Spirit is moving. It's also important to know what not to do. Some people can flow flawlessly in the Spirit. Other folks have no knowledge of the Spirit whatsoever, so it's up to the office gifts to equip the people. Never assume people have the knowledge of proper operation in Spiritual gifts just because they attend church.

Did you know that someone must facilitate and manage a service where the Spirit is moving? A spiritual overseer will keep watch while the prophetic and supernatural is happening. Some may think that there is no need for oversight when God is moving. Unfortunately, that is not the case at all. I told our recent class that spiritual services can be my most stressful services. They met that statement with blank stares, so I'll explain it to you as I did to them. When the Spirit moves through others in our services, I immediately become a facilitator. I am watchful that everything flows properly without disruption or confusion. The pastor, the worship team and all the congregation must flow together with the Holy Spirit. Someone must be the watchman and it's not always fun. For one thing, you don't get to fully participate because you're making sure everything goes smoothly. It's my job to make sure those couple of people who try to interrupt don't. It's my job to make sure those working in the anointing are free from distraction. Those services are amazing, but I don't always get to participate. I get to manage the movement. Either myself or the overseers have to keep watch to insure the Spirit flows freely. Now think about your wonderful band members, your singers, your media personnel and your ushers. Unless the Spirit is flowing through them they are alert and on standby like the overseers. The wonderful praise team that brought you into the presence of God, they man their post to ensure the flow continues while everyone else enjoys the atmosphere. Not to say they can't be involved, but usually not to the extent of the people. You know what I'm talking about if you've ever experienced Spirit filled services. Now, if the spiritual movement happens through me it's a different story. I'm involved while other overseers man the post. It's wonderful when you get to participate rather than facilitate. Every move of God requires someone to pastor the prophetic. If you don't lead and train others to lead, chaos will generally erupt, either intentionally or unintentionally. The better the people are trained the less you need to worry.

There is an orderly way and an unorderly way things happen. The Holy Spirit is a perfect gentleman, disruption is never His fault. He will never cause a person to act out of order. No matter how many times they say the Spirit made me do it, He does not cause confusion. If confusion, disruption or competition ever take place, it is the fault of the person. The result of a proper Spirit filled service is overwhelming peace and joy. The result of a chaotic service is frustration. I've facilitated both. I'm happy to report that I've had a life full of amazing spiritual experiences.

Allow me to give you some personal out of order experiences. In all these situations, I or an appointed elder had to pastor the prophetic and bring correction. Sometimes I can sense the Spirit preparing to move and I'll announce a waiting on the Lord. Just then multiple people want to come and give me their input on direction. Now, there's a good time to do that and a horrible time. A good time is when I'm clearly not searching, a bad time is when I'm seeking the Lord for guidance, and someone pecks on my shoulder to give input. Why would you interrupt the one person who just announced, the Spirit is preparing to move, and I will now seek Him? We once had a sweet lady who would let out an ear-piercing hurdling scream every few minutes during our spiritual services. That had to be stopped immediately. She quickly told me that she couldn't control it and without hesitation, I quickly told her that she had no choice. I've witnessed more prophetic words, or tongues with interpretation, given in a service than biblically allowed. People attempting to give a so-called word from the Lord while fumbling and stuttering, searching for what to say. Folks waiting for an opportune time during a service to pull out the notes from their weekly prayer time to share. Their attempt was to give it as a fresh word. Then you have the pain of people answering phones or allowing phones to ring during services. People waiting for a move of the Spirit, so they can take their bathroom break and walk back and forth in the isles. The rudeness of people usurping authority and abruptly taking command of a service. People with the inability to give silent reverence during a quiet or meditating time. Those people who wait for a brief moment of silence, so they can do their deed. Then you have the excessively loud prayers that over power the entire room. Folks who always think they should meet and pray with anyone who edges away from their seat. I sometimes want to say, I'm having one on one time with God, get off my back. Folks operating outside their anointing and their calling. Sound tech's suddenly deciding to experiment with the sound while the Spirit is moving. Band members who want to rock and roll when the Spirit wants reverence. Someone breaking into an ill-timed testimony to discuss their weekly troubles. And every church has that one person who goes around talking to everyone they perceive is not participating in the moment. Don't make eye contact, they'll come to you next. The list could go on and on. If you attend church long enough, you'll witness people doing things disorderly and out of place. But praise God, the good definitely outweighs the bad. You now understand why someone must pastor the prophetic. Unfortunately, the lack of knowledge in proper protocol must be governed. I've also witnessed God move in spectacular ways. When He's not disrupted, I've witnessed powerful salvations, healings, miracles and upper room type revivals. I've witnessed and experienced being slain in the Spirit. I've witnessed and participated in people being set free from demonic spirits. I've seen the proclaimed dead come to life. I've witnessed lives restored, marriages restored, and churches restored. More times than I can count, the presence of God saturates a place when believers know how to allow the Spirit to move without disruption or disorder.

When I was young and under my parent's ministry, I considered them hero's. They were anointed to identify and expel demons, among many other things. I remember my first time experiencing this. Not long after this event started you could see that several people had no idea the importance of what was happening. They seemed to care less. My dad rose from the floor, temporarily leaving his post, and pastored the prophetic. He boldly announced the seriousness of the situation. He then said, "you are either assisting or your leaving, but you will not sit in here and be disruptive. If your unconcerned, leave. If your anointed, pray." Then he went back to his post and completed the work.

Jesus had a similar experience.

(John 12:1-8 NKJV) *"Then, six days before the Passover, Jesus came to Bethany, where Lazarus was who had been dead, whom He had raised from the dead. There they made Him a supper; and Martha served, but Lazarus was one of those who sat at the table with Him. Then Mary took a pound of very costly oil of spikenard, anointed the feet of Jesus, and wiped His feet with her hair. And the house was filled with the fragrance of the oil. But one of His disciples, Judas Iscariot, Simon's son, who would betray Him, said, "Why was this fragrant oil not sold for three hundred denarii and given to the poor?" This he said, not that he cared for the poor, but because he was a thief, and had the money box; and he used to take what was put in it. But Jesus said, "Let her alone; she has kept this for the day of My burial. For the poor you have with you always, but Me you do not have always."*

Even Jesus had to shepherd prophetic movements. In this case, a rebuke with correction was necessary. Rebuke is not done to embarrass. It's done to teach and train those who have acted out of order. Judas was interrupting something that he had nothing to do with, nor did he understand or care. He was more interested in his own cares and personal gains. This text speaks of an act that was necessary, but it was unannounced to those in attendance. The Spirit is spontaneous and moves without notice. Jesus knew the purpose of the anointing of His body and it became necessary for Him to pastor those in attendance.

Spiritual movements don't just happen seamlessly. Every Spirit-filled church requires the offices of the fivefold ministry to teach, train and equip the people for such times. If the Spirit moves freely in your church, thank your pastor and your leaders because they have done a great job at pastoring the prophetic.

The Apostle Paul's writings teach more than any other regarding the Spirit, and how to operate in Him and His gifts. We must distinguish whether his writings were for that particular church or the church as a whole. The reason for this needed distinction is because some things were for particular times and particular churches. Other things Paul wrote was for the entire body, past and present. Many of his letters were addressed to churches he oversaw. For example, he wrote to the church at Corinth, to the church in Galatia and to the church of Ephesus. Many of his letters were to establish order and proper function. No one is given freedom to roam without covering. Every Christian and every gift needs to be under the accountability and equipping of the fivefold ministry. The prophetic moving of the Holy Spirit must have a shepherd.

(1 Corinthians 12:1 NKJV) *"Now concerning spiritual gifts, brethren, I do not want you to be ignorant."*

(1 Corinthians 14:32–33 NKJV) *"32 And the spirits of the prophets are subject to the prophets. 33 For God is not the author of confusion but of peace, as in all churches of the saints.*

(1 Corinthians 14:40 NKJV) *"Let all things be done decently and in order."*

We have a repeated concern that all things be done in order, not chaotically without covering. Ignorance will reveal itself, but proper training will prevail and benefit the body. Confusion is never the fault of the Spirit. Confusion and disorder are beyond His ability. Some will attempt to blame their failure on Him, "He made me do it." The above Scripture says the gifts are subject to the container or carrier of the gifts. The Spirit will not overtake and bully you. Disruption and chaos are a byproduct of ignorance. Let all things be done decently and in order. When we operate in the Spirit, we are putting Him on display. It needs to be the best display this world has ever seen. If we do it right, we will be His representatives in love, forgiveness and reconciliation. His best awaits you.

The purpose of God breathing on you is to radically change your life and to radically change those around you. He seeks to be your identity. He seeks to enable you to change the world.

When God the Father breathes, it brings life.

When God the Son breathes, it brings salvation.

When God the Holy Spirit breathes, it brings power.

Have all three breathed on you? Has the Father breathed life into your being? Has the Son breathed salvation in you? Has the Holy

Spirit breathed on you, releasing heaven's power? If so, you now represent Him. You represent Him in the Father, the Son, and the Holy Spirit. You are life – You are salvation – You are power. May it be on earth as it is in heaven.

When God Breathes
To God be the glory!

Printed in the United States
By Bookmasters